KT-365-058

TIDINGS
of COMFORT
& JOY

TIDINGS
of COMFORT
& JOY

*A Christmas Feast
of Faith & Fun*

Pam Rhodes

HODDER &
STOUGHTON

First published in Great Britain in 2015 by Hodder & Stoughton
An Hachette UK company

1

A CIP catalogue record for this title is available from the British Library

ISBN 978 1 473 63003 1
eBook ISBN 978 1 473 63005 5

Typeset in Sabon MT by Hewer Text UK Ltd
Printed and bound in the UK by Clays Ltd, St Ives plc

Hodder & Stoughton policy is to use papers that are natural, renewable
and recyclable products and made from wood grown in sustainable
forests. The logging and manufacturing processes are expected to
conform to the environmental regulations of the country of origin.

Hodder & Stoughton Ltd
Carmelite House
50 Victoria Embankment
London
EC4Y 0DZ

www.hodderfaith.com

Contents

Whatever life has brought your way,
I wish you love on Christmas Day,
Laughter, peace, contentment too,
All blessings that I wish for you.

Pam

Introduction

Hallelujah or Ho Ho Ho?

We wish you a merry Christmas,
We wish you a merry Christmas,
We wish you a merry Christmas
And a happy New Year!
Glad tidings we bring
To you and your king,
We wish you a merry Christmas
And a happy New Year!

(Sixteenth-century traditional carol)

Merry Christmas, everyone!

Or is it?

Are you like a big kid, full of excited anticipation the moment you hear in the middle of September that there are only one hundred shopping days left until Christmas? Or does that very thought have you digging out your 'Bah Humbug!' sign from the loft so that you can display it prominently in the front garden? Or maybe yours is the garden that becomes a wonderland of twinkling lights depicting Santa's grotto, Christ in the manger and reindeers parked on the rooftop?

Are you that well-organised person who elbows their way through the crowds to snap up bargains in the January sales, so that you can have your Christmas presents wrapped and neatly stacked in the cupboard before the decorations come down on Twelfth Night? Or are you rushing into shops as the doors are about to close on Christmas Eve, desperate for inspiration as you *start* gift-hunting for your nearest and dearest?

Are you a traditional 'roast turkey, stuffing and three veg' sort of cook – or do you prefer to graze on chocolate and Turkish delight all day? Is your homemade pudding ready and waiting in the larder by the end of November, and your cake being drip-fed brandy for weeks before marzipan and icing gets anywhere near it? Do you go on a diet to prepare for over-eating at Christmas – or overeat at Christmas knowing your annual resolution is to eat nothing at all for the whole month of January?

Does Christmas seem crackers to you? Or does the whole idea of that season of present-giving, party-going, card-sending and festive singing warm your heart during the dark days of winter?

Whatever your attitude to Christmas, amid all the frantic build-up to the festive season do you ever find yourself longing for more? In our throwaway, get-it-instantly, hi-tech twenty-first-century world, does your soul reach out for simple and eternal truth? Is the story of a baby being born in a stable in Bethlehem just the stuff of Christmas cards and songs to you, or do you find yourself wondering about this child whose birth is still celebrated two thousand years later? What is the truth about him – and what does that truth mean for you today?

Our Christmas today only exists because of the birth of Jesus. The meaning, promise and glory of that time when God came to dwell on earth with us remain at the heart of all our celebrations. But our Christmas season has expanded and blossomed way beyond that simple truth. Nowadays, those who profess to no faith at all join Christians in giving gifts, sending greetings cards and decorating their homes as friends share their time and families gather together. This book encompasses all of that, and I hope it will be read and enjoyed on many different levels. It's stuffed like a Christmas stocking with everything from wonder to whimsy – Advent wreaths, nativity plays, carol singing and ding-dong bells nestling comfortably alongside sparkling lights, holly and mistletoe, traditions and recipes, the presents under the tree and the fairy perched on top! Dip into any page and you're likely to find something that recalls a memory, makes you smile, touches your heart or lifts your soul. I found, as I wove all these thoughts together, that I was moved to tears on occasions, laughing out loud at others and bursting into song without the need for any hymn book as I joined in with carols we know so well!

These truly are 'tidings of comfort and joy'. I hope they warm and inspire you – both the hallelujah and the ho ho ho!

The Word became Flesh

In the beginning was the Word, and the Word was with God, and the Word was God. He was with God in the beginning. Through him all things were made; without him nothing was made that has been made. In him was life, and that life was the light of all mankind. The light shines in the darkness, and the darkness has not overcome it.

The true light that gives light to everyone was coming into the world. He was in the world, and though the world was made through him, the world did not recognise him. He came to that which was his own, but his own did not receive him. Yet to all who did receive him, to those who believed in his name, he gave the right to become children of God – children born not of natural descent, nor of human decision or a husband's will, but born of God.

(John 1:1-5, 9-13)

I

Does Christmas Matter?

Though Christ a thousand times
In Bethlehem be born,
If he's not born in me
My heart is all forlorn.

(Anonymous)

Why on earth should something which happened in a little town in Judea more than two thousand years ago be of any interest to us in our lives today? What is it about the birth story of a baby who wasn't famous, rich or obviously noteworthy that has made it so enduring?

The power of that story was made clear to me in the most humbling way a couple of years ago when I was lucky enough to be one of the leaders on a pilgrimage trip around the Holy Land. It's a fascinating, and often very emotional, experience to visit those places whose names we've known all our lives from stories in the Bible. But if you've ever been on such a trip, you'll know it can be completely exhausting too, as there are so many sites to see in a short space of time. You're forever climbing off and on the coach, tearing around one significant location after another at breakneck speed, and no pilgrim wants to miss out on any of them!

There were about fifty of us travelling on our coach, and I soon became aware of an undercurrent of exasperation among some of the group about a delightful but quite elderly lady, Phyllis. She was cheerfully struggling to keep up with the rest of us but going at such a slow pace that some were grumbling she was holding up the whole party. It was clear, though, that she just couldn't walk any faster, not because she was disabled in any way, but for the simple reason that she was wearing the most inappropriate shoes – huge open-toed leather flip-flops that seemed to be several sizes too big for her. No wonder she had to take her time walking over the uneven surfaces in the ancient places we were visiting!

Finally, the inevitable happened. While we were wandering around the town of Bethlehem she lost her footing and took a nasty tumble, though it left her shaken rather than hurt. For the rest of the afternoon, I kept her company as we meandered around, leaving the others in the group to make the rounds much more speedily without us to hold them back.

As we walked, she told me her story. This pilgrimage was something she'd dreamed of doing for years, and when she finally booked it, she'd bought a place not just for herself, but also for her son, because they really wanted to share the experience together. Tragically, soon after the tickets arrived, he developed a severe form of cancer, and by the time the trip came around, he was far too ill to travel. So she decided to take him with her by wearing his shoes, so that she could walk in the footsteps of Christ for him.

What faith! What love! And what inspired such faith and love in her was the sense of fellowship she felt with another mother in Bethlehem from two thousand years earlier. That young mother also gave birth to a son she loved; taught and cared for him as he grew; felt pride in his achievements as a young man – and she too knew the pain that one day she would have to watch him die.

Phyllis had no doubt that the baby born in Bethlehem all that time ago was the Messiah, the Son of God – but her heart went out to Mary, a mother facing a similar sense of grief as Phyllis was facing herself two thousand years on. She believed that Mary's maternal love and faith was all she had to comfort her as she watched her son die on the cross – but because Jesus rose again to fulfil God's eternal will, the same hope and reassurance Mary had in the knowledge that her son was now seated with God in heaven could be shared by Phyllis too. Because of Christ, her son would also be in the care of the God she loved. For Phyllis, there was immense comfort in that.

So when she put on her own son's shoes to walk in the footsteps of Christ, she was accepting God's will for her family. Christ did that too, from his birth, throughout his life and ministry, beyond his death, to be the living God he is to Phyllis and all Christians today.

That's why his birth two thousand years ago still matters – and that's why people around the world continue to celebrate his coming each year with joy and thanks.

Love Came Down at Christmas

Love came down at Christmas,
Love all lovely, love divine;
Love was born at Christmas,
Star and angels gave the sign.

Worship we the Godhead,
Love incarnate, love divine;
Worship we our Jesus:
But wherewith for sacred sign?

Love shall be our token,
Love be yours and love be mine,
Love to God and to all men,
Love for plea and gift and sign.

(Christina Rossetti, 1830–94)

2

When was the First Nowell?

It came upon the midnight clear,
That glorious song of old,
From angels bending near the earth,
To touch their harps of gold;
'Peace on the earth, goodwill to men,
From Heaven's all-gracious King.'
The world in solemn stillness lay,
To hear the angels sing.

(Edmund Sears, 1810–76)

'It came upon a midnight clear', we are told – but when, exactly? Was it in fact 25 December in the year from which we start counting our calendar today?

Scholars down the centuries have come up with all sorts of theories about when Christ was actually born, but while absolute certainty is impossible, several major clues can be found in the Bible story itself.

First, we're told that shepherds were in the fields watching their flocks at the time of Christ's birth. December is cold and rainy in Judea, so the shepherds would have kept their flocks sheltered at that time of year, rather than out in the fields.

Their being out in the fields suggests that Jesus was born in mid- to late summer.

Second, we learn that Jesus' parents went to Bethlehem to register in a Roman census. As temperatures may well have dropped below freezing in winter and roads at that time were very poor, it would have been a hopeless exercise to try and organise a census in the winter, since it would involve people travelling long distances across country. But these negative indications don't really help us pin anything down.

So to try and pinpoint the probable time of Christ's birth, biblical scholars take their clues from events which are easier to calculate. Luke tells us that John's mother, Elizabeth, was in the sixth month of her pregnancy when Jesus was conceived. The question is, when was John born? Well, his father, Zechariah, was a priest serving in the Jerusalem temple during the course of Abijah, which was known to be in the middle of June. During the time of his temple service, Zechariah learned that he and his wife would have a child, and it was after he'd travelled home from his stay in Jerusalem that John was conceived. If that happened towards the end of June, adding nine months brings us to the end of March as the most likely time for John's birth. The age difference between John and Jesus, we are told, was six months – which suggests that the most likely time for Christ's birth was the end of September.

Next question: what year was Christ born? Using information from the Bible once again, we learn from Matthew that Jesus was born during the days of Herod the king, who died in 4 BC. We then learn that Herod ordered that all boys in Bethlehem of two years old and younger should be killed, which means that Jesus could have been as old as two before

Herod's death. That would place the date of his birth between 6 and 4 BC.

Another clue comes from the first two verses of Luke Chapter 2: 'In those days Caesar Augustus issued a decree that a census should be taken of the entire Roman world. (This was the first census that took place while Quirinius was governor of Syria.)' We know that Caesar Augustus reigned from 27 BC to AD 14 and that Quirinius was governing Syria during this same time period. There are records of a census being taken in approximately 6 BC which included Judea. Based on these historical details, it seems most likely that Christ was born in Bethlehem between 6 and 5 BC.

This fits with what we know about the end of Christ's life, too. Luke tells us at the start of a long list of fathers and sons in Chapter 3 of his Gospel, verse 23, that Jesus began his ministry when he was about thirty years old. We know too that his ministry began during the time when John the Baptist was in the wilderness – according to the first two verses of Luke Chapter 3 this started 'In the fifteenth year of the reign of Tiberius Caesar – when Pontius Pilate was governor of Judea, Herod tetrarch of Galilee, his brother Philip tetrarch of Iturea and Traconitis, and Lysanias tetrarch of Abilene – during the high-priesthood of Annas and Caiaphas'.

The only time period that fits all of these facts is AD 27–29. If Jesus was 'about thirty years of age' in AD 27, that would fit with his birth being sometime between 6 and 4 BC. More specifically, Jesus would have been approximately thirty-two years old at the time he began his ministry.

So, historical and biblical facts suggest that Jesus was probably born in Bethlehem in Judea in late summer, in either 6 or 5 BC.

The *next* question is, why do we celebrate the fact of his birth on 25 December? It was Pope Julius I who chose that date to represent Christ's birthday. He did this, though, not because he thought the date was accurate, but because it falls near to the shortest day of the year, when many people in different countries were already celebrating winter festivals – in particular the Roman festival of Saturnalia when Saturn, the god of the harvest, was honoured. And across Northern Europe, during the festival of Yule, giant logs were trimmed with ribbons and green plants, then burned to the gods in the hope that the sun would shine more brightly. So, the timing of those pagan festivals became the opportunity for Christians around the world to celebrate the birth of their Lord.

But, whenever he was actually born and however we have chosen to mark that fact down the years, what is certain is that his birth changed history forever, along with the lives of countless generations of people around the world. The words of this next poem by Godfrey Rust capture perfectly how those momentous events of long ago happened quietly and almost without notice.

The Shepherds

It was done plainly enough.
The night sky was a perfect billboard,
the sound effects spectacular.

Only a few were awake
and in the right place
at the right time when heaven,
unable to contain its amazement any longer,

spilled out momentarily into earth
and explained itself.

The message was clear as day
but his timing was, as always, surprising,
and the show ran
for one performance only.

(Godfrey Rust)

When a vicar went along to talk to five-year-olds about why Joseph and Mary had to travel to Bethlehem before their baby was born, he mentioned the census held in order to levy taxes. He obviously thought five-year-olds had a greater understanding of the tax system than most adults I know! Later, when the class teacher asked the children if they knew why Mary and Joseph needed to make the journey to Bethlehem, a little girl in the front row stuck up her hand and said, 'They had to go and see about their cactus.'

There is a real poignancy about the much-loved carol 'It came upon the midnight clear', the first verse of which introduced this section. In a world burdened with intolerance, selfishness, suspicion and worry – both then and now – the birth of yet one more baby can seem insignificant. And yet, in the coming of the Christ-child, there is promise, joy and hope for all, as you'll see from the rest of the verses.

It came upon the midnight clear,
that glorious song of old,
from angels bending near the earth
to touch their harps of gold:
'Peace on the earth, good will to men
from heaven's all-gracious King!'
The world in solemn stillness lay
to hear the angels sing.

Still through the cloven skies they come,
with peaceful wings unfurled;
and still their heavenly music floats
o'er all the weary world:
above its sad and lowly plains
they bend on hovering wing;
and ever o'er its Babel-sounds
the blessed angels sing.

Yet with the woes of sin and strife
the world has suffered long;
beneath the angel-strain have rolled
two thousand years of wrong;
and man, at war with man, hears not
the love-song which they bring:
O hush the noise, ye men of strife,
and hear the angels sing.

When was the First Nowell?

For lo, the days are hastening on,
by prophet-bards foretold,
when, with the ever-circling years,
comes round the age of gold;
when peace shall over all the earth
its ancient splendours fling,
and the whole world give back the song
which now the angels sing.

(Edmund Sears, 1810-1876)

3

Sugar and Spice and All Things Nice

For we all like figgy pudding,
We all like figgy pudding,
For we all like figgy pudding,
So bring some out here!

(Traditional)

Whatever the facts are about *why* we celebrate Christmas, it's enough for most of us to know that every December we can look forward to the sheer joy of this most wonderful time of the year! Before we know it, the big day is just a few weeks away – and that's the time when, for me, the great challenge is to knuckle down to my first traditional job of the season: making the Christmas pudding and cake. Correction – I should say 'puddings and cakes', because over the years I've discovered that being able to give neighbours and friends a homemade pud or a rich fruit cake is really appreciated. If you've ever had proper homemade offerings, rather than the ones bought in the supermarket, you'll discover that in the taste stakes, they are in a league of their own!

At this point, I have to admit that all through the thirty or so years that I have regularly been making as many as a dozen puddings and Christmas cakes in all shapes and sizes, I have had one constant companion in the kitchen. I've never met Delia Smith, but I reckon most households in Britain have one of her cookery books on a shelf in the kitchen. My own copy is dog-eared and covered with splodges from various meals and desserts I've attempted in the past – but, in my humble opinion, her recipes for both Christmas cake and puddings are foolproof even for the absolute beginner.

Over the years my family have become used to avoiding the kitchen on 'Pudding Day', because the whole room ends up looking like an old-fashioned laundry with all its windows steamed up, as just about every pot I possess bubbles away for around eight hours while I cook the puddings. The process starts the night before, when my arms have come close to falling off from the effort of mixing together huge quantities of dried fruit, suet, breadcrumbs, apples, lemon and orange peel, along with dozens of eggs and generous glugs of rum, stout and barley wine. The mix is left overnight so that the flavours can mellow into each other, ready to be put into pudding pots and tied up with muslin and string the next day before cooking.

Years ago, families would have been eating 'plum porridge' rather than the pud we know now. It was an odd dish with a rather alarming variety of ingredients – the usual breadcrumbs, raisins, currants, wine and spices we know, but with beef and mutton broth added! It wasn't eaten as a dessert with lashings of delicious brandy butter and cream, but was spooned on to the plate along with the meat course. Plum porridge went out of fashion in the late eighteenth century, though, to be replaced by a much stiffer mix, more like the pudding we know today.

Mind you, along the way that old killjoy Cromwell and his Puritans added insult to injury by beheading King Charles I, then pronouncing a ban on all saints' days, even Christmas, outlawing mince pies, decorations like holly and ivy – and plum puddings! It was a ruling that was hard to enforce, though, and I'm sure many a pudding was secretly munched behind closed doors before, at the restoration of the monarchy in 1660, the legislation from Cromwell's time was declared null and void and Christmas could be openly celebrated again. Thank goodness for that!

They say that the earlier you make the puddings, the more delicious they'll be. In fact, some people keep leftover puds from the previous year, claiming that a whole twelve months of being kept in a cool, dark cupboard enhances the flavour no end! Traditionally, though, the day to start cooking was the Sunday nearest to St Andrew's Day, 30 November. It became known as 'Stir Up Sunday', because of the collect for that day which says, 'Stir up, we beseech Thee, O Lord, the wills of thy faithful people.'

There are other traditions surrounding the Christmas pudding, too. It should be stirred with wood, as a reminder of the wooden manger – and stirred 'sunwise' (or clockwise) to copy the Magi's route from the East. Lastly, for luck, all the family should take their turn. Three wishes go to each stirrer, although it's said that only one wish will be granted. There is also a custom that there should be exactly thirteen ingredients in the pudding, representing Jesus and the apostles.

I can certainly remember my grandmother putting little silver charms in the pudding – and if you were lucky enough to find one in your portion, it gave you an idea of what the coming year would bring. If you came across a ring, a marriage would follow; a button meant bachelorhood; a thimble brought disappointment, because it meant the girl who found it would remain an 'old maid', and a silver sixpence was good luck.

There's also an old wives' tale that if you eat Christmas pudding in thirteen different houses before the first day of the New Year, you will have exceptional joy. That's my kind of challenge!

Into the basin put the plums,
Stir-about, stir-about, stir-about!

Next the good white flour comes,
Stir-about, stir-about, stir-about!

Sugar and peel and eggs and spice,
Stir-about, stir-about, stir-about!

Mix them and fix them and cook them twice,
Stir-about, stir-about, stir-about!

(Traditional rhyme, anonymous)

But enough about puddings! It's time for cake . . .

The crowning glory of the big Christmas bake-up is surely the traditional Christmas cake, with its rich fruit and spice mix soaked in brandy before cooking, then drip-fed brandy for weeks after its four hours in the oven, so that the moment you cut into the marzipan and thick royal icing that covers it the aroma of rich, fruity, spiced brandy tickles your nose and has you grabbing for a plate!

Back in the sixteenth century, all cakes would have been boiled because few people had the luxury of any sort of oven – so 'cake' and 'pudding' would have been much the same thing. Once richer families started to have ovens in the home, the Christmas cake emerged, with its heady mix of dried fruit and spices which were symbolic of the spiced gifts brought by the Magi. Because of this connection with the Three Kings, this cake was usually saved until Epiphany, earning it the nickname of Twelfth Night cake.

It was Victorian bakers who started to decorate seasonal cakes with royal icing, winter snow scenes and Father Christmas characters. I'm not alone in my struggle every year to create something artistic for our Christmas cake. Fortunately, I am able to come up with a variation on the theme because Richard, my husband, has a Christmas Day birthday – so I always make him a traditional iced fruit cake smothered in marzipan and icing, then top the lot with birthday greetings – and the odd robin or holly leaf thrown in!

To be honest, I prefer my fruit cake without all that sugary topping. None of the rest of the family shares my taste, though, so each year I make one cake just for me, piled high with colourful fruits – raisins, sultanas, apricots, cherries, orange and lemon peel as well as almonds and walnuts, all coated in shiny apricot jam glaze. Delicious!

North of the border, the Scottish Dundee cake is a favourite, with no decoration on top but generous helpings of whisky soaked into the cooked cake before the big day. Equally, I rather like the tradition in Yorkshire of teaming up fruit cake with a tasty bit of cheese, perhaps a nice chunk of Wensleydale. Yum!

We have started to adopt some Continental favourites in more recent years, of course. The German Stollen is becoming popular in Britain – a drier, pale-coloured cake properly called Weihnachtsstollen. And panettone from Italy is a familiar sight here as well, not just at Christmas but all year round. This rich bread, with its distinct cupola shape, is traditionally eaten during the Christmas season, with raisins and candied citrus fruit. Meanwhile, in France, the chocolate Yule Log, or Bûche de Noël, is generally the preferred choice of the French, rather than any sort of fruit cake.

Further afield, they love cake in India too, often giving spicy fruit Allahabadi cakes as gifts. In Japan, they prefer a sponge cake which is usually eaten on Christmas Eve, frosted with whipped cream and decorated with strawberries and seasonal chocolates.

Christmas cakes in the Philippines are bright yellow pound cakes covered in nuts and fruit soaked in brandy or rum and mixed with palm sugar syrup. They add interesting flavours like civet musk, rose or orange water. The cakes have to be soaked in copious amounts of alcohol because they need to stay fresh for many months after they're baked. At least, that's what they say. I think they just like boozy cake!

Whatever it's made of, and whatever it tastes like, the more important question is, how soon can you cut it? In Victorian times, it was thought to be unlucky to cut the cake before dawn on Christmas Eve. The only problem is that, over the following few days, both the Victorians *then* and all of us *now* are in the habit of eating far too much!

Who has room for rich fruit cake once we're stuffed with turkey, pudding, roast ham, chocolate treats and salted nuts?

Me! I shouldn't – but I always do!

My great friend Lynn belongs to the Ladies' Guild at her church, a group which rallies round with enthusiasm whenever there's any work to be done or funds to be raised. In early

December, under the instruction of Margaret, their formidable 'Chair', they organise a Christmas cake sale to raise money for the hampers which the church distributes to people in the community who are struggling to put food on the table at Christmas.

As much as Lynn enjoys making cakes, last year she was working long and demanding hours at her office. On the Friday night before the cake sale the following morning, she came home exhausted. The last thing she felt like doing was baking a cake! All the same, she knuckled down to the job – although her heart plainly wasn't in it, because when the cake emerged from the oven, it certainly wasn't the golden-brown, beautifully domed masterpiece she usually came up with. Quite the opposite: it sagged completely in the middle and looked dreadful!

Always resourceful, after a moment's thought Lynn turned the cake over, dug out the mix in the middle, stuffed the cavity with rolled-up kitchen paper, turned the whole thing upright again – and iced it beautifully! Then, as she drove down to the church to drop her cake off in the porch ready for the morning, she called into her daughter's house on the way to show her what she'd done before making a heartfelt plea.

'Please would you make sure you are first in the line when the door of the church hall opens at ten tomorrow?' she begged. 'Find this cake and buy it before anyone realises what I've done!'

At five past ten the next morning, her daughter rang her.

'I couldn't find the cake anywhere!' she said anxiously. 'I was definitely the first one through the door when the sale opened, but it must have been snapped up immediately before I spotted it!'

In the end, Lynn realised she couldn't do a thing about it,

so she just had to hope that whoever bought the cake had no way of identifying her as the cook!

It was traditional during that first weekend of December for the Ladies' Guild to gather at the formidable Margaret's house for Sunday afternoon tea as a prelude to the Christmas season. None of the ladies ever missed it. With Margaret in charge, nobody dared!

It was the usual decorous affair as the ladies sat around chatting, sipping tea, munching tiny sandwiches, canapés and sweet treats. But Lynn had no sooner walked in than her attention was drawn to the magnificent spread that had been provided. She gasped in horror: there, in pride of place right in the middle of the table, was her cake!

As her knees buckled beneath her, she managed to sink on to a chair at the side of the room while she desperately wondered what to do. She would have to own up, of course. She couldn't possibly allow Margaret to face the embarrassment of cutting the cake in public. That would be unthinkable. Full of apprehension at the prospect of confessing, she slowly got to her feet planning to move quietly around to where Margaret was standing alongside the table.

At just that moment, a lady from the other side of the room called across, 'Margaret, this buffet is absolutely wonderful. And that cake! It's beautiful!'

'Thank you,' said Margaret, graciously accepting the compliment. 'I made it myself!'

There is a God, thought my friend, as she quietly slid back into her seat.

I think I would have liked Helen Maria Williams. That might surprise you a little because this educated English woman, born in the eighteenth century, was a very serious-minded writer and poet. It was often through poetry that she expressed her blunt political views both in England and later in Paris, which became her home. Her outspoken comments frequently got her into trouble and eventually landed her in prison in Luxembourg – which she didn't mind too much, as she was at least allowed to carry on writing.

But across the years, I feel quite a sense of sisterhood with her. Why? Because of Christmas cake! When she received the gift of a homemade Christmas cake at her Paris home, baked and sent by a friend in England, it seemed to encompass for her both the twinge of homesickness she often felt, and her gratitude and wonder at the love and thoughtful friendship that had gone into making the gift. Being a poet, she for once abandoned more serious subjects and poured out her feelings about Christmas cake in beautiful verse!

So, as I stand for hours in a steam-filled kitchen making dozens of Christmas cakes and puddings, most of which I will wrap up for family members and old friends, I find myself echoing her thoughts. You can say a lot without words in a cake!

To Mrs K—, On Her Sending Me an English Christmas Plum-Cake at Paris

What crowding thoughts around me wake,
What marvels in a Christmas-cake!
Ah say, what strange enchantment dwells

Enclosed within its odorous cells?
Is there no small magician bound
Encrusted in its snowy round?
For magic surely lurks in this,
A cake that tells of vanished bliss;
A cake that conjures up to view
The early scenes, when life was new;
When memory knew no sorrows past,
And hope believed in joys that last! –
Mysterious cake, whose folds contain
Life's calendar of bliss and pain;
That speaks of friends for ever fled,
And wakes the tears I love to shed.
Oft shall I breathe her cherished name
From whose fair hand the offering came:
For she recalls the artless smile
Of nymphs that deck my native isle;
Of beauty that we love to trace,
Allied with tender, modest grace;
Of those who, while abroad they roam,
Retain each charm that gladdens home,
And whose dear friendships can impart
A Christmas banquet for the heart!

(Helen Maria Williams, 1761–1827)

4

Dashing Through the Snow

'Twas the night before Christmas, when all through the house
Not a creature was stirring, not even a mouse . . .

Clement Clark Moore was an American professor of divinity, who is said to have written this poem for his children on 23 December 1822. He really started something, with his affectionate, colourful tale of a jolly, fur-clad, chubby old elf who sweeps through the sky before guiding his sleigh and eight reindeer (each individually named) on to the roof of a house. Slinging a bundle onto his back he squeezes his rotund frame down the chimney to find that the children there had left stockings hanging up for him to fill with toys from his sack. Then, with a knowing wink, a finger to one side of his nose and a nod, he disappears back up the chimney, jumping on to the sleigh with a whistle to set the reindeer off and up into the starry sky.

A Visit from St. Nicholas

'Twas the night before Christmas, when all through the
*   house*
Not a creature was stirring, not even a mouse;

The stockings were hung by the chimney with care,
In hopes that St. Nicholas soon would be there;
The children were nestled all snug in their beds,
While visions of sugar-plums danced in their heads;
And mamma in her 'kerchief, and I in my cap,
Had just settled our brains for a long winter's nap,
When out on the lawn there arose such a clatter,
I sprang from the bed to see what was the matter.
Away to the window I flew like a flash,
Tore open the shutters and threw up the sash.
The moon on the breast of the new-fallen snow
Gave the lustre of midday to objects below,
When what to my wondering eyes did appear,
But a miniature sleigh, and eight tiny reindeer,
With a little old driver, so lively and quick,
I knew in a moment it must be St. Nick.
More rapid than eagles his coursers they came,
And he whistled, and shouted, and called them by
*   name;*
'Now, Dasher! now, Dancer! now, Prancer and Vixen!
On, Comet! on, Cupid! on, Donner and Blitzen!
To the top of the porch! to the top of the wall!
Now dash away! dash away! dash away all!'
As leaves that before the wild hurricane fly,
When they meet with an obstacle, mount to the sky;
So up to the house-top the coursers they flew,
With the sleigh full of toys, and St. Nicholas too.
And then, in a twinkling, I heard on the roof
The prancing and pawing of each little hoof.
As I drew in my head, and was turning around,
Down the chimney St. Nicholas came with a bound.

He was dressed all in fur, from his head to his foot,
And his clothes were all tarnished with ashes and soot;
A bundle of toys he had flung on his back,
And he looked like a pedlar just opening his pack.
His eyes – how they twinkled! his dimples how merry!
His cheeks were like roses, his nose like a cherry!
His droll little mouth was drawn up like a bow
And the beard of his chin was as white as the snow;
The stump of a pipe he held tight in his teeth,
And the smoke, it encircled his head like a wreath;
He had a broad face and a little round belly
That shook when he laughed, like a bowl full of jelly.
He was chubby and plump, a right jolly old elf,
And I laughed when I saw him, in spite of myself;
A wink of his eye and a twist of his head,
Soon gave me to know I had nothing to dread;
He spoke not a word, but went straight to his work,
And filled all the stockings; then turned with a jerk,
And laying his finger aside of his nose,
And giving a nod, up the chimney he rose;
He sprang to his sleigh, to his team gave a whistle,
And away they all flew like the down of a thistle,
But I heard him exclaim, ere he drove out of sight
'Happy Christmas to all, and to all a good-night!'

(Clement Clarke Moore, 1779–1827)

Before this poem became famous, children around the world would not have recognised the character described here – Father Christmas, or Santa Claus, as we think of him today. St Nicholas, though, was familiar around the world because, back in the Middle Ages, he was a popular saint, patron of merchants, sailors, parish clerks, scholars, pawnbrokers and small boys!

Not a lot is known about the real Nicholas, except that he was reputed to have been the Bishop of Myra in Asia Minor during the fourth century. His reputation for kindness is better known than the reasons *why* he gained such acclaim for being a warm-hearted, caring man. One story is that in his home town lived a father who was so poor he couldn't even afford to feed his three daughters, let alone provide them with the dowries they needed to make a good marriage. Wanting to help, but without making his generosity known, Nicholas dropped a bag of gold under cover of night down the chimney of the house, where it fell into a shoe or stocking which the eldest daughter had placed in the hearth to keep warm. Some say that's why children still hang up their stockings or leave a shoe out so that St Nicholas can fill it with toys. He did the same for the two younger girls in the family, but eventually he was discovered by the grateful father, who was duly sworn to secrecy. I guess he wasn't very good at keeping secrets because Nicholas was eventually made a saint, with the day of 6 December dedicated to honouring him.

In Amsterdam on that day, tradition holds that St Nicholas arrives by boat before mounting a white horse to make his rounds. By his side are Moorish servants, all in sixteenth-century Spanish dress, and Black Peter, St Nicholas's right hand man. For centuries, Black Peter had been known to accompany 'the gift-giver' who appeared in the traditional stories of many different countries. Some said that Black Peter was, in fact, the Devil, who had been tamed by St Nicholas. If the saint had any doubts about the behaviour of a particular child, it was Black Peter's job to dole out his or her punishment!

The current custom in Amsterdam is that St Nicholas and his helpers throw out gingerbread to the crowd, church bells ring, bands play and all the great and the good come along to welcome the saint to their city. That evening everyone in Holland gives gifts to those they love – but those gifts should always have an element of surprise. It may be a tiny present hidden in a huge box, or a wrapped parcel secreted where it's hard to find – anything that makes the occasion as happy a surprise as St Nicholas's first presents were said to have been.

In parts of Germany, Switzerland, Holland, Belgium and Austria, St Nicholas's Day is also known as 'children's day', and is almost considered to be more important than Christmas Day itself. Shops are full of marzipan fruits and animals, gingerbread and toys. Sometimes parents dress up as St Nicholas, who is said to set much store on whether children have been 'good' or 'bad'. On the evening before St Nicholas's Day, children put out shoes and clogs full of hay for the saint's white horse, and perhaps a glass of schnapps for Black Peter – anything to sweeten his opinion of them if they aren't certain they've been *quite* good enough!

Christmas Toys

What will you find in your stockings,
Good little girls and boys?
Horses and donkeys and trumpets,
Lots of wonderful toys!

Dolly in lovely dresses,
Tops, and a sword and gun;

Rattles, and jacks in boxes,
Jolliest things for fun!

Play-houses, bows and arrows,
Turkeys and ducks that squeak,
Candies, and tiny tea sets,
Baa-lambs wooly and meak.

Old Santa will surely bring us
Some of these wonderful toys,
Oh, Christmas he always remembers
Good little girls and boys.

(Anonymous)

In Iceland, any children who have doubts about whether they've behaved well enough should be quaking in their shoes as Christmas approaches. The old tradition there is that the Jolasveinar Christmas spirits or trolls come down from the mountains bringing gifts – but only for those who've been good!

Otherwise they'll make mischief. There's Stiff-Necked Sheep-Chaser; Gorge Oaf, who steals milk from idle dairy-maids; Shorty, who heads for kitchen pans so that he can lick them clean; the Sausage-Stealers, who will pinch any smoked meats they can find; Sniffer, whose nose leads him to the pets' bowls from which he can help himself to their food; the Candle-Beggar, who steals candles left burning at night; and the Meat-Hooker, who reaches down chimneys to grab racks of meat!

Most terrifying of all the night trolls is Gryla, who, with her husband and large family, are said to control the Christmas festivities by staying close to the family birch rod. Parents may still warn their troublesome children with the old saying, 'If you land in Gryla's bag at Advent, you will be in the soup at Christmas!'

Terrifying!

Down the years, children everywhere have bubbled with excitement at the thought of what gifts Father Christmas might leave for them. Of course, sometimes their expectations are alarmingly high, which can be quite a problem for mum and dad.

Some old friends of mine have a delightful five-year-old who came up with a long list of presents she wanted Father Christmas to organise. With loving tactfulness, her parents explained that it might not be possible for Santa to bring *everything* she wanted.

Their daughter thought for a moment, then said, 'OK! I'll have to ask Gentle Jesus then.'

A good time is coming, I wish it were here,
The very best time in the whole of the year;
I'm counting each day on my fingers and thumbs
The weeks that must pass before Santa Claus comes.
Then when the first snowflakes begin to come down,
And the wind whistles sharp and the branches are brown,

I'll not mind the cold, though my fingers it numbs,
For it brings the time nearer when Santa Claus comes.

(Anonymous)

In an 1863 edition of *Harper's Illustrated Weekly*, a drawing by Thomas Nast was featured. Instead of showing the familiar image of St Nicholas in a long, dark-red hooded robe trimmed with fur, this figure was in bright red with a wide leather belt and round fur hat with a sprig of holly in it! It was Thomas Nast who called this figure 'Santa Claus' – and in some ways he went back to his Bavarian roots as he dreamed up the character we all know so well. His Santa Claus was short, paunchy and rather gnomish, with a crimped beard and a long-stemmed pipe, which he smoked while he waited on the rooftop for children to go to sleep. Thomas could probably remember growing up with memories of the European 'gift-bringer', who often arrived by horse or dog team (or occasionally by camel), and it seems he translated that memory into a sleigh and reindeer. A legend was born!

So, where does Santa go on Christmas Day when his rounds of gift-giving are done and he's ready to put his feet up for a bit until he needs to get started on preparations for next year? Well, the Swedes, Icelanders, Finns and Greenlanders all lay claim to the secret location where Santa and his elves live in a snowbound log cabin complete with extensive workshop. Certainly, most children I know will tell you without any doubt that Santa's home is to be found in the icebound land-scape of the Arctic Circle.

But some people don't need snow and ice to share the magic. In the hills of south Indiana, there's apparently a town called Santa Claus which has roads named Kriss Kringle Street, Christmas Tree Lane and Three Kings. The local lakes are named Christmas, Noel and Holly – and to greet visitors to the town, there's a huge painted statue of Santa Claus that weighs in at forty-two tons! Only in America . . .

Some of you may know that I presented evening television news programmes for many years – and I think I would really have enjoyed reading out the report on this mysterious case!

The Christmas Eve News

Good evening.

The police authorities are hopeful that tonight they will finally get to the bottom of their longest-standing unsolved mystery – the case of the serial present-giver Father Christmas, also known as Santa Claus.

Inspector Hunch of Scotland Yard said that the police have, with the use of an advanced computer programme, found a pattern to the break-ins by this intruder and are confident that he will strike again tonight.

Inspector Hunch went on to add that members of the public should not be unduly alarmed by the likelihood of a break-in and stressed that although the strange intruder always leaves gifts, he has never been known to take anything other than the odd mince pie and a tipple from the drinks cupboard.

To assist the police with this investigation, in shopping centres all over the country, reconstructions have been staged with the help of Father Christmas look-alikes performing the act of giving. It is hoped that these reconstructions might jog the memories of members of the public with any information which might help unmask the mystery giver.

Father Christmas is described as tallish, heavily bearded and athletic, although overweight. He is said to dress in a red suit and matching bobble hat. The police advise all members of the public who witness Father Christmas in the act of leaving gifts in their bedrooms to be asleep but urged them to phone Scotland Yard as soon as the intruder has left the scene of the generosity.

Now, the Christmas Eve weather. Under tonight's brightly shining moon, deep snow is expected of the crisp and even kind. A cruel frost is expected later.

That is the end of the news.

Good night.

(Philip Waddell)

So, the old 'gift-giver', first known as St Nicholas, later Father Christmas and then Santa Claus, is still the caring character who rewards our thoughtful deeds with gifts at Christmas. For the rest of the year, he's preparing for his next annual visit at his home in the snowy Arctic.

It's odd how often (in the words of the song) we find ourselves 'dreaming of a white Christmas'! In all honesty, I don't think I can remember more than one or two years when there's been even a flurry of snow on Christmas Day. Nevertheless, our Christmas cards often depict traditional scenes of snow, icicles, robins and winter berries. Even in our carols, we allow ourselves to imagine the stable in Bethlehem in the depths of snow. That's certainly the image created by a much-loved Christmas hymn which was chosen as the nation's favourite carol a few years ago. The words started life in 1850 as a poem by Christina Rossetti, whose father, Gabriele, had fled to London to escape the authoritarian regime in his native Naples. You'd have thought that, with her Italian blood, Christina would have imagined the crib scene in Middle East warmth – and yet this poem begins with lines that describe the frosty chill of deep winter.

Christina Rossetti never knew how her words came to touch so many, as her text wasn't discovered until after she died in 1894 – but by 1906, it had appeared in *The English Hymnal* set to a haunting melody by Gustav Holst. Maybe it's the music, perfectly paired with the words, that makes it so special. Or perhaps it's simply the four lines of the last verse, which touch the hearts of all of us with their simple expression of faith and humility.

In the Bleak Mid-winter

In the bleak mid-winter
Frosty wind made moan,
Earth stood hard as iron,
Water like a stone;
Snow had fallen, snow on snow,
Snow on snow,
In the bleak mid-winter
Long ago.

Our God, Heaven cannot hold Him
Nor earth sustain;
Heaven and earth shall flee away
When He comes to reign:
In the bleak mid-winter
A stable-place sufficed
The Lord God Almighty,
Jesus Christ.

Enough for Him, whom cherubim
Worship night and day,
A breastful of milk
And a mangerful of hay;
Enough for Him, whom angels
Fall down before,
The ox and ass and camel
Which adore.

Angels and archangels
May have gathered there,
Cherubim and seraphim
Thronged the air,
But only His mother
In her maiden bliss,
Worshipped the Beloved
With a kiss.

What can I give Him,
Poor as I am?
If I were a shepherd
I would bring a lamb,
If I were a wise man
I would do my part,
Yet what I can I give Him,
Give my heart.

(Christina Rossetti, 1830–94)

After those beautiful verses, which paint an evocative picture of the birth of Christ as bleak yet full of wonder, I'm afraid I'm going to lower the tone a bit. The following little poem about winter weather goes down very well with my grandson, who especially enjoys the last line!

Snowball

I made myself a snowball,
As perfect as could be.
I thought I'd keep it as a pet
And let it sleep with me.

I made it some pyjamas
And a pillow for its head,
Then last night it ran away,
But first – it wet the bed!

(Shel Silverstein)

One of my favourite writers is Derek Dobson, who has the knack of creating verse and prose alike which is simple to read and easy on the senses – yet, after a while, I always find that something in his choice of phrase and thought has gone much deeper. Most of all, I like the way in which his lines always strike a chord in me, making every word relevant – and often very challenging.

A Christmas Snowflake

A cold snowflake drifts down from the white sky above totally oblivious as to what awaits at the end of its journey. That lonely pure white flake settles gently on a window pane. As the warmth from within the house permeates through the glass, the snowflake melts from what was cold, lifeless and without feeling into a tear that gently runs down the window.

Leo Buscaglia once said, 'Too often we underestimate the power of a touch, a smile, a kind word, a listening ear, an honest compliment, or the smallest act of caring, all of which have the power to turn a life around.'

This Christmas, let that snowflake tear of compassion become your act of kindness; for whatever you do for another can never be measured. The cost to you will be nothing, yet to another it could be a priceless gift.

(Derek Dobson)

The Promise

The people walking in darkness
have seen a great light;
on those living in the land of deep darkness
a light has dawned.
For to us a child is born,
to us a son is given,
and the government will be on his shoulders.
And he will be called
Wonderful Counsellor, Mighty God,
Everlasting Father, Prince of Peace.
Of the greatness of his government and peace
there will be no end.
He will reign on David's throne
and over his kingdom,
establishing and upholding it
with justice and righteousness
from that time on and forever.
The zeal of the LORD Almighty
will accomplish this.

(Isaiah 9:2, 6, 7)

5

Light in Our Darkness

Like a candle flame
Flickering small in our darkness
Uncreated light
Shines through infant eyes

God is with us, alleluia
God is with us, alleluia
Come to save us, alleluia
Come to save us, alleluia!

(Graham Kendrick)

I don't know about you, but after the clocks go back at the end of October, I feel a bit as if I'm 'living in a land of deep darkness', just as the reading from Isaiah describes. Then when December comes in, the lights come out! Almost overnight our towns, streets and houses are transformed into a winter wonderland of glistening sparkle. Lights twinkle along the lines of every rooftop, shine in front windows, decorate shrubs in gardens, hang in strings across the town square and beckon enticingly from every shop window.

Like a candle flame
Flickering small in our darkness
Uncreated light
Shines through infant eyes

God is with us, alleluia
God is with us, alleluia
Come to save us, alleluia
Come to save us, alleluia!

Stars and angels sing
Yet the earth sleeps in shadows
Can this tiny spark
Set a world on fire?

Yet his light shall shine
From our lives, Spirit blazing
As we touch the flame
Of his holy fire

God is with us, alleluia,
Come to save us, alleluia!

(Graham Kendrick)

In every neighbourhood, there's always an impressively organised enthusiast with the vision and the electrical know-how to cover every inch of their home and garden with Christmassy scenes – Rudolph and his flashing red nose, or Santa climbing up and down a ladder calling 'Ho, ho, ho!' Sometimes there will be an illuminated stable complete with the baby in the manger and a sheep or even a donkey, if you're lucky. Often, though, they don't bother with the original Christmas story at all because it's nowhere near as visual as the Seven Dwarfs, a Tinkerbell or two and a brightly lit sleigh which seems to take off into the sky one minute, then land back where it started the next. And so the spectacle continues, all night and every night for the five weeks or so of the Christmas period.

Please don't think for one moment that I'm sniffy about the way our lives quite literally light up as Christmas approaches! I love it! I'm the one who screeches to a halt outside any house that's covered in schmaltzy sparkles – often to the great annoyance of the drivers behind me! That kind of over-the-top decoration has such an air of celebration, community and warm-hearted fun – it gives pleasure to even the most casual onlooker. I know some may feel that we're following in the wake of our American cousins, who really do go overboard with lights at Christmas – but does it matter, when it brings such brightness and joy? And for those who grumble that it's all a commercial ploy, far removed from the truth of Christmas itself, well, of course it is – but if it weren't for the wonderful story of Christ's birth, there would be no Christmas, and no excuse to decorate our towns so gloriously during the darkest days of winter.

The one thing I dread about lights at Christmas, though, is the effect they have on my husband, Richard. A bit like the Incredible Hulk, he comes over all possessive and controlling once the boxes of Christmas lights have come out of the loft. The gangly strings of lights soon stretch out right down the hall and around a corner or two, so that he can sort out which strings are working, and which innocent-looking bulbs are actually dastardly devils preventing hundreds of others from bursting into life as they should! Richard's lip curls and his eyes turn red if any member of the family dares even to *look* at the lights, let alone *touch* or *move* any of them. If he runs out of time to finish his thorough check of each bulb, those strings of lights might lie there for days, even weeks. I remember one Christmas Eve, I and the rest of the family were anxiously waiting for him to give us permission to start decorating the tree while we stood around holding the boxes of baubles and tinsel, along with the family's much-loved fairy who is *always* lovingly placed on the highest bough of our tree.

At least, we think she's a fairy. My daughter, who made her at school when she was nine years old, can't remember whether her colourful creation was intended to be a fairy or an angel. She has got wings, so she *could* be a fairy – but she also has the remains of a silvery crown (or is it a halo?) on the tatty shreds of yellow wool that pass for her hair, which might mean she's really an angel, which is how I like to think of her. Mostly, though, we all just know that once she is placed with great triumph at the top of the lit and decorated tree, Christmas has come and all is well with the world!

Anyway, back to my story – you remember, about Richard and his curling lip and his possessive obsession with fairy lights? We had been waiting with boxes at the ready for a fortnight or more, in the hope that he would finally be satisfied that he'd placed the strings of lights in exactly the right positions on the trees we wanted to decorate around the house. We'd begun to wonder if we might miss Christmas altogether and end up decorating the trees on Boxing Day when he'd eventually managed to complete The Grand Lighting Plan!

Is this a 'man thing'? Do other families find the same – that the lovely man who is just 'Dad' all through the year, becomes a bad-tempered demon who takes the 'cheer' out of 'cheerful' when it comes to what should be the joyful task of putting up Christmas lights?

However, somehow we survive the ordeal every year and eventually there comes the magical moment when the lights are switched on, brightening up every corner as only they can – or at least, as Dad's Lighting Masterplan dictates that they should!

The Fairy on the Christmas Tree

The fairy on the Christmas tree
Is looking quite forlorn.
Her wand is broken and splinted;
Her wings, all tattered and torn.
Her dress of stiff crepe paper
Was once a bright sky blue,
But time has bleached it all away.
It's now a much paler hue.
But through it all, each Christmas
She sits in pride of place,
Gazing down on the proceedings,
A serene smile on her face.
She sat there when I was growing up,
And when my son was small,
And, somehow, I know she'll still be there

When the grandchildren come to call.
She's become a part of my family life,
Of memories which I hold dear,
And to me, at least, she heralds in
A Christmas filled with cheer.
And I just can't bear to give her up,
To heartlessly throw her away.
To me she represents Christmases Past
And she will to my dying day.

(Dawn Ferrett)

Every year as I hang tinsel around our Christmas tree, I am reminded of a lovely story I was told as a child. In reality, there can be little truth in it, but there is something reassuring about this tale of danger, despair and unexpected help from a very unlikely source.

After the visit by the Magi, Joseph had a dream in which an angel of the Lord appeared to him, to warn him that Herod was searching for their son, and wanted to kill him. Before long, the family heard that Herod was ordering that all boys under the age of two in Bethlehem and the surrounding area should be killed. They packed up their meagre possessions and fled immediately in the hope of finding safety.

The story goes that, on the first evening, they were exhausted and cold, as the ground was covered in a crisp, white frost. After a while, Joseph spotted a cave which would at least give them shelter from the weather, even though Herod's men might still spot it and realise it could be a good hiding place.

The cave looked empty, but in fact it was already occupied by a little spider who was very worried when he saw the baby inside the freezing cave. He wished he could do something to keep the little boy warm during the long, cold night. So he set about doing what he could do best. He started to spin a fine, silvery web, inch by inch, until at last it stretched right across the cave's entrance. On and on he worked so that eventually there was a thick curtain of silky web blocking access to the cave.

He finished just in time because, before long, a detachment of Herod's soldiers climbed up the path, looking to fulfil Herod's bloodthirsty order.

They noticed the cave and quickly climbed up to inspect it – but just as they were about to burst in to see if anyone was hiding there, the captain noticed the spider's web. It was covered with white frost and stretched right across the entrance.

'Well, that's it!' he said. 'This spider's web has been here for days. There can't be anyone hiding in this cave or the web would have been ripped apart.'

And that, so they say, is why we put tinsel on our Christmas trees – as a reminder of the frosty web that saved the lives of Mary, Joseph and their precious son.

And they owed it all to a little spider who had no idea of the scale of what he'd just done . . .

The Gospel Tree

There once was a shining Christmas tree
Standing out where all could see.
Its brilliance captured every eye
And seemed to cheer each passer-by.

'The lights are so bright,' they would say
And hesitate to walk away.
The tree stood proud, ablaze with light
For every light was burning bright.

Then one bulb was heard to say
'I'm tired of burning night and day;
I think I'll just go out and take a rest
For I'm too tired to do my best;

Besides I am so very small
I doubt if I'd be missed at all.'
Then a child lovingly touched the light,
'Look, mother, this one shines so very bright.

I think of all the lights upon the tree
This one looks the best to me.'
'Oh my goodness,' said the light
'I almost dimmed right out of sight.

I thought perhaps no one would care
If I failed to shine my share.'
With that a glorious brilliance came
For every light had felt the same.

Our Gospel, like this Christmas tree,
With little lights which are you and me,
We each have a space that we must fill
With love, and lessons and good will.

Let's keep our tree ablaze with light,
With testimonies burning bright.
For our Gospel is a living tree
That lights the way to eternity.

(Tafadawa Mhondiwa Mugari)

Three trees stood together, dreaming and talking as they grew on the hillside. The first tree wished to be cut down and made into a baby's cradle. The second wished to be made into a wonderful ship carrying rich goods and precious jewels. The third didn't particularly wish to be cut down, but just wanted to go on growing on the hillside, pointing its branches up to heaven.

As time passed, the woodcutters came along, and the tree which had wanted so much to be made into a cradle became a cattle stall. And it was there that Jesus was born.

The second one, which had wished to be a splendid ship, was cut down and made into a small fishing boat which was eventually lent to Jesus by Simon Peter so that he could speak from it to the people on the shores of Galilee.

And the third, which had just wanted to go on growing, had to be cut down because it was needed for a cross of shame.

But it was the cross on which Christ the Saviour of the world died – the same Christ who was the babe in the cattle stall; the same Christ who taught from Simon Peter's boat.

In a few short paragraphs that old folk tale about the three trees reflects on some poignant and pivotal moments in Christ's life. And bearing in mind how much beauty and atmosphere all Christmas trees bring into our homes, I like the idea of each of those trees growing on a hillside, dreaming of who will choose it, and what role it will have to play.

If I were a pine
With needles lean,
If I were a fir
With branches green,
Do you know what
I'd want to be?
A shimmering, shining
Christmas tree.

(Anonymous)

Here's a hymn with words so old that no one quite knows who wrote them, although it's said that they may have been sung and even danced to during three-day Cornish religious festivals which took place many years ago.

The verses were 'collected' by William Sandys, a lawyer who had a passionate interest in old verse and the music that accompanied it. In 1833, he'd unearthed enough old verses to bring out a book of carols, which he divided into three sections. The title of the first section was 'Ancient Carols and Christmas Songs from the early part of the fifteenth century to the end of the seventeenth century'. The last part of the book was dedicated to French provincial carols – but the middle section was filled with forty carols 'still used in the West of England'.

If it weren't for William Sandys and his hobby of collecting old songs, we might never have heard of 'I Saw Three Ships', 'God Rest You Merry, Gentlemen', or even 'The First Nowell'. We would also have missed out on a beautiful old hymn, 'Tomorrow Shall be my Dancing Day' which, in much more detail than my previous short story about the three trees, traces the life, death and resurrection of Christ in the form of a touching, rhythmic carol.

> *Tomorrow shall be my dancing day;*
> *I would my true love did so chance*
> *To see the legend of my play,*
> *To call my true love to my dance;*
>
> *Chorus: Sing, oh! my love, oh! my love, my love, my love,*
> *This have I done for my true love.*

Then was I born of a virgin pure,
Of her I took fleshly substance;
Thus was I knit to man's nature
To call my true love to my dance.

In a manger laid, and wrapped I was
So very poor, this was my chance
Between an ox and a silly poor ass
To call my true love to my dance.

Then afterwards baptized I was;
The Holy Ghost on me did glance,
My Father's voice heard I from above,
To call my true love to my dance.

Into the desert I was led,
Where I fasted without substance;
The Devil bade me make stones my bread,
To have me break my true love's dance.

The Jews on me they made great suit,
And with me made great variance,
Because they loved darkness rather than light,
To call my true love to my dance.

For thirty pence Judas me sold,
His covetousness for to advance:
Mark whom I kiss, the same do hold!
The same is he shall lead the dance.

Before Pilate the Jews me brought,
Where Barabbas had deliverance;
They scourged me and set me at nought,
Judged me to die to lead the dance.

Then on the cross hanged I was,
Where a spear my heart did glance;
There issued forth both water and blood,
To call my true love to my dance.

Then down to hell I took my way
For my true love's deliverance,
And rose again on the third day,
Up to my true love and the dance.

Then up to heaven I did ascend,
Where now I dwell in sure substance
On the right hand of God, that man
May come unto the general dance.

(William Sandys, 1792–1874)

The Fall

Now the snake was more crafty than any of the wild animals the LORD God had made. He said to the woman, 'Did God really say, "You must not eat from any tree in the garden"?'

The woman said to the snake, 'We may eat fruit from the trees in the garden, but God did say, "You must not eat fruit from the tree that is in the middle of the garden, and you must not touch it, or you will die."'

'You will not certainly die,' the snake said to the woman. 'For God knows that when you eat from it your eyes will be opened, and you will be like God, knowing good and evil.'

When the woman saw that the fruit of the tree was good for food and pleasing to the eye, and also desirable for gaining wisdom, she took some and ate it. She also gave some to her husband, who was with her, and he ate it. Then the eyes of both of them were opened, and they realised they were naked; so they sewed fig leaves together and made coverings for themselves.

Then the man and his wife heard the sound of the LORD God as he was walking in the garden in the cool of the day, and they hid from the LORD God among the trees of the garden. But the LORD God called to the man, 'Where are you?'

He answered, 'I heard you in the garden, and I was afraid because I was naked; so I hid.'

And he said, 'Who told you that you were naked? Have you eaten from the tree that I commanded you not to eat from?'

The man said, 'The woman you put here with me – she gave me some fruit from the tree, and I ate it.'

Then the LORD God said to the woman, 'What is this you have done?'

The woman said, 'The snake deceived me, and I ate.'

(Genesis 3:1-13)

6

The First Winter

Adam lay ybounden,
Bounden in a bond;
Four thousand winter
Thought he not too long.

If ever a loving husband and wife are going to fall out, odds are it will be at Christmas time. This 'season of goodwill' is fraught with relationship pitfalls as the big day approaches. There always seems to be too much to do and so little time to do it!

But then, the whole story of Christmas stems from a relationship tussle between the very first husband and wife, Adam and Eve. The hymn 'Adam lay ybounden' recalls the story we've just read in Genesis of Adam and Eve eating forbidden fruit in the Garden of Eden. And don't you think the way in which each blamed the other is all too familiar from our own family squabbles today? In the end, God was so angry at both their actions and their attitude that he banished them from the Garden forever. That banishment lasted, according to this old hymn, for four thousand winters.

Adam Lay Ybounden

Adam lay ybounden,
Bounden in a bond;
Four thousand winter
Thought he not too long.
And all was for an apple,
An apple that he took,
As clerkës finden written
In their book.
Nor had one apple taken been,
The apple taken been,
Then had never Our Lady
A-been heaven's queen.
Blessed be the time
That apple taken was.
Therefore we may singen
Deo gratias!

(Fifteenth century, anonymous)

These words came from a fifteenth-century manuscript, probably written during the reign of Henry V, who died in 1422.
The dialect within the words suggests it originated in the East
Anglian county of Norfolk, and the original may have
belonged to a wandering minstrel because another of the
poems on the same page in the manuscript is entitled 'A
Minstrel's Begging Song'. In those days, there was a belief
that, because of his disobedience in committing that original
sin, Adam was destined to remain 'in bonds' (which seems to

mean 'in limbo') from the time of his death until 'four thousand winters' later – when, at his crucifixion, Christ took upon himself the sins of the world.

Unusually for religious songs of this time, these words are disarmingly human, revealing much about the writer. Whoever he was, he was plainly astonished that such devastating punishment should be given when 'all was for an apple'! He thinks it must be true, though, because he knew the 'clerks' found it in 'their book' – which probably refers to the Vulgate, a Latin translation of the Bible written by St Jerome in 352.

The third verse suggests that the birth of Jesus Christ to Mary is an act of redemption for man, and that Mary would become Queen of Heaven because of her role as Christ's mother. And the song then ends on a positive note, suggesting that the eating of the apple was a blessed fault, because of the happy consequence of Christ's birth on earth.

Perhaps that's something to bear in mind when arguments bubble up within the family around Christmas. Sometimes grievances have to be aired, and our own part in causing hurt to others acknowledged and forgiven. After many a good argument comes the even better experience of making up again – and that can be quite refreshing and reassuring for all involved.

The effect of Adam's 'transgression' on subsequent generations comes at the start of another old hymn, 'A Virgin Unspotted', which was probably written about two centuries later than 'Adam Lay Ybounden'. And, like that previous text, this hymn also sees great joy and celebration in the birth of Christ bringing release from the bondage of past failings.

A Virgin Unspotted

A virgin unspotted, the prophet foretold,
Should bring forth a Saviour, which now we behold,
To be our Redeemer from death, hell and sin,
Which Adam's transgression entangled us in.

Chorus: Now let us be merry, put sorrow away:
Our Saviour, Christ Jesus, was born on this day.

At Bethlehem city in Jewry, we know,
That Joseph and Mary together did go,
And there to be tallied with many they came,
Since Caesar Augustus commanded the same.

But when they had entered the city so fair,
A number of people so mighty was there,
That Joseph and Mary, whose substance was small,
Could find in the inn there no lodging at all.

Then they were constrained in a stable to lie,
Where horses and asses they used for to tie:
Their lodging so simple they took it no scorn,
Before the next morning our Saviour was born.

The King of all kings to this world having come,
They sought out fine linen to wrap Him in some,
And when she had swaddled her young Son so sweet,
Within an ox manger, she laid Him to sleep.

Then God sent an angel from Heaven so high,
To certain poor shepherds in fields where they lie,

66

And bade them no longer in darkness to stay,
Because that a Saviour was born on this day.

Then presently after the shepherds did spy
Vast numbers of angels that covered the sky;
They joyfully cried out and sweetly did sing,
To God be all glory, our heavenly King.

To teach us humility all this was done;
We learn haughty pride and resentment to shun:
A manger His cradle who came from above,
The great God of mercy, of peace, and of love.

(Mid-seventeenth century, anonymous)

Christmas is a good time to think about the ways in which we might have sinned against each other. The message of Christmas is of love, peace and promise, and even those who aren't Christians find themselves caught up in the business of showing their care for others in the form of cards and presents.

Mind you, sometimes those cards and gifts are more an act of duty than love, which seems a shame. Often we only make contact with the people on our card list at Christmas, and may never be in touch with them at any other time throughout the year. And occasionally the thought occurs to us that we end up buying presents for each member of the family or our circle of friends simply because that's the way it's always been, and that's what we're expected to do.

Around the beginning of December, the season of Advent begins – the four weeks leading up to Christmas when we prepare for the coming of Christ. It can be a very busy time as we rush around buying presents, wrapping, writing cards, visiting friends to make deliveries and rushing to the Post Office in the hope that we haven't missed the last deadline for posting!

But Advent can also be a time of reflection – about the year that's past, the people who have been important to us, and our part in all that's happened. Have we felt hurt by the uncaring attitude of others? Perhaps. But if so, how have we treated them?

So often, our own treatment of other people is reflected in their responding attitude to us. When we're caught up in the busyness of our own lives, simple expressions of care and connection can get lost. Actions speak louder than words. A Christmas card once a year doesn't make a friendship. Allowing time for each other, being a good listener, remembering what is important in the lives of others, being trustworthy, offering a helping hand for which no reward is expected or wanted – that's what makes loving relationships and lasting friendships.

Poor old Adam paid dearly for his selfish deed. Four thousand winters in limbo! The least we can do is to give some honest thought to our own selfishness and how it might have impacted on others around us. And then, remember the power of little words like 'sorry' and 'thank you' when they are sincerely meant. You might be surprised at the effect using those words can have – how just acknowledging out loud your gratitude or your desire for forgiveness can start to unravel the knot of resentment and anger which all too often festers within us.

So make your first thought for Advent one of looking back as well as looking *forward*; looking not just at those around you, but at yourself too.

The Fall

From the very beginning
nothing was ruled out
and nothing ruled in
except choice,
but every choice
rules out another.

And so we are excluded
from the garden.
Pain is included.
Only love and its sacrifice
remains a choice
without limitation.

(Godfrey Rust)

Formerly a school inspector in the Yorkshire Dales, Gervase Phinn has the most delightful sense of humour, deep insight and an excellent memory for tiny but poignant moments. Those qualities, among others, have helped him to become a bestselling author. This is a little poem from his book *Twinkle Twinkle, Little Stars* that made me chuckle.

Bible Class

Reverend Bright, our vicar,
Came to our class today.
He started with a little talk,
Then we closed our eyes to pray.
He talked about the Bible,
And the prophet Abraham,
How God created everything
And how the world began.
Then he asked us all some questions
About the prophets and the kings,
David and Goliath,
And lots of other things.
'In a very famous garden
Grew an apple on a tree,
And who ate the forbidden fruit?'
And a voice said:
'Wasn't me!'

(Gervase Phinn)

The Birth of John the Baptist Foretold

In the time of Herod king of Judea there was a priest named Zechariah, who belonged to the priestly division of Abijah; his wife Elizabeth was also a descendant of Aaron. Both of them were righteous in the sight of God, observing all the Lord's commands and decrees blamelessly. But they were childless because Elizabeth was not able to conceive, and they were both very old.

Once when Zechariah's division was on duty and he was serving as priest before God, he was chosen by lot, according to the custom of the priesthood, to go into the temple of the Lord and burn incense. And when the time for the burning of incense came, all the assembled worshippers were praying outside.

Then an angel of the Lord appeared to him, standing at the right side of the altar of incense. When Zechariah saw him, he was startled and was gripped with fear. But the angel said to him: 'Do not be afraid, Zechariah; your prayer has been heard. Your wife Elizabeth will bear you a son, and you are to call him John. He will be a joy and delight to you, and many will rejoice because of his birth, for he will be great in the sight of the Lord. He is never to take wine or other fermented drink, and he will be filled with the Holy Spirit even before he is born. He will bring back many of the people of Israel to the Lord their God.

And he will go on before the Lord, in the spirit and power of Elijah, to turn the hearts of the parents to their children and the disobedient to the wisdom of the righteous – to make ready a people prepared for the Lord.'

Zechariah asked the angel, 'How can I be sure of this? I am an old man and my wife is well on in years.'

The angel said to him, 'I am Gabriel. I stand in the presence of God, and I have been sent to speak to you and to tell you this good news.'

(Luke 1:5-19)

7

The Messenger

Saint John was like a flaming torch,
Evangelist of coming light,
Forerunner of the reign of grace,
And messenger of truth's full light.

By birth he came before the one
In whom both God and man combine,
And in due time he did baptise
The very source of life divine.

As Christ who came to save the world
Did conquer through a death of shame,
So too the Baptist shed his blood
To seal the work for which he came.

Most tender Father, grant us grace
In John's straight way our feet to keep,
That nurtured in the living Christ
Eternal joys we too may reap.

(The Venerable Bede, 673–735)

These ancient words, translated relatively recently by the Benedictine nuns of St Cecilia's Abbey in Ryde on the Isle of Wight, were written by the Venerable Bede who, back at the start of the eighth century, lived right up at the top end of England near Durham. Bede is considered to be one of the greatest of all the Anglo-Saxon scholars, a man who was constantly fascinated by history and science. To him, God was in everything. Every scrap of creation was of God. God is the source of all science and present in every moment both of history and the future.

With these words, Bede describes the essential part played by John the Baptist in the story of Christ. His mother Elizabeth and Mary, mother of Jesus, were friends, although Elizabeth was considerably older, beyond the normal age of child bearing. It is in the nature of women, even today, that they turn to their friends to share the whole experience of being pregnant and becoming a parent. These two women shared a special bond beyond just friendship. Both of them had been told by an angel that the child they were carrying had a special role to play in God's plan for mankind.

Later, Christ described John as a 'messenger', sent ahead to prepare the way for him. In fact, John's role was foretold seven centuries before by the prophet Isaiah who spoke of: 'A voice of one calling: "In the wilderness prepare the way for the Lord; make straight in the desert a highway for our God"' (Isaiah 40:3).

You can just imagine the impression John made on people who knew him as he grew up and took on what must have seemed a very eccentric lifestyle, which was simple to the point of basic. He wore little more than a camel's hair garment with a leather belt, and generally shunned places where there were crowds, choosing instead to spend most of his time in the desert which stretched about twenty miles east from Jerusalem and Bethlehem down to the Jordan River and the Dead Sea. But there was plainly something very charismatic about him, because hundreds, perhaps even thousands, flocked to see him in the hope that they would be immersed in the River Jordan by this man who became known as 'John the Baptist'. Even Christ himself came to be baptised, reuniting these two men whose lives had been linked by God's will long before their two mothers shared their uncertainty along with their wonder at the first news of their pregnancy.

On Jordan's Bank the Baptist's Cry

On Jordan's bank the Baptist's cry
Announces that the Lord is nigh;
Awake and hearken, for he brings
Glad tidings from the King of kings!

Then cleansed be every Christian breast,
And furnished for so great a guest!
Yea, let us each our heart prepare
For Christ to come and enter there.

For thou art our salvation, Lord,
Our refuge, and our great reward;
Without thy grace we waste away
Like flowers that wither and decay.

To heal the sick stretch out thy hand,
And bid the fallen sinner stand;
Shine forth, and let thy light restore
Earth's own true loveliness once more.

All praise, eternal Son, to thee
Whose advent sets thy people free,
Whom, with the Father, we adore,
And Holy Ghost, for evermore.

(Charles Coffin, 1676–1749 translated
John Chandler, 1806–1876)

John the Baptist was born six months before Christ. If we could imagine Jesus the baby growing within his mother's womb, what would his thoughts have been? That was a question that occurred to the much-admired Welsh writer, R. S. Thomas, a man of devout faith. In his poem 'The Coming', he imagines God allowing his Son a glimpse of the world to which he was coming:

The Coming

And God held in his hand
a small globe. Look, he said.
The son looked. Far off,

The Messenger

as through water, he saw
a scorched land of fierce
colour. The light burned
there; crusted buildings
cast their shadows: a bright
serpent, a river
uncoiled itself, radiant
with slime.
On a bare
hill a bare tree saddened
the sky. Many people
held out their thin arms
to it, as though waiting
for a vanished April
to return to its crossed
boughs. The son watched
them. Let me go there, he said.

(R. S. Thomas, 1913–2000)

The Birth of Jesus Foretold

In the sixth month of Elizabeth's pregnancy, God sent the angel Gabriel to Nazareth, a town in Galilee, to a virgin pledged to be married to a man named Joseph, a descendant of David. The virgin's name was Mary. The angel went to her and said, 'Greetings, you who are highly favoured! The Lord is with you.'

Mary was greatly troubled at his words and wondered what kind of greeting this might be. But the angel said to her, 'Do not be afraid, Mary; you have found favour with God. You will conceive and give birth to a son, and you are to call him Jesus. He will be great and will be called the Son of the Most High. The Lord God will give him the throne of his father David, and he will reign over Jacob's descendants forever; his kingdom will never end.'

'How will this be,' Mary asked the angel, 'since I am a virgin?'

The angel answered, 'The Holy Spirit will come on you, and the power of the Most High will overshadow you. So the holy one to be born will be called the Son of God. Even Elizabeth your relative is going to have a child in her old age, and she who was said to be unable to conceive is in her sixth month. For no word from God will ever fail.'

'I am the Lord's servant,' Mary answered. 'May your word to me be fulfilled.'

Then the angel left her.

(Luke 1:26-38)

8

People Get Ready

The Angel Gabriel from heaven came,
his wings as drifted snow, his eyes as flame;
'All hail,' said he, 'thou lowly maiden Mary,
most highly favoured lady.'
Gloria!

'For know, a blessèd mother thou shalt be,
all generations laud and honour thee,
thy Son shall be Immanuel, by seers foretold;
most highly favoured lady.'
Gloria!

Then gentle Mary meekly bowed her head,
'To me be as it pleaseth God,' she said,
'My soul shall laud and magnify his holy name':
most highly favoured lady.
Gloria!

Of her, Immanuel, the Christ was born
in Bethlehem, all on a Christmas morn,
and Christian folk throughout the world will ever say,

Tidings of Comfort and Joy

'Most highly favoured lady.'
Gloria!

(Basque Carol, Charles Bordes [collector], 1863–1909,
Sabine Baring-Gould, 1834–1924)

Sabine Baring-Gould, writer of the hymn 'Onward Christian Soldiers', wrote this familiar Advent hymn which has taught many generations of children about the angel Gabriel's visit to Mary, the mother of Jesus.

There is something so touching about this young girl, Mary, as she humbly accepts the incredible message she receives – from an angel, no less! The news that she, who was not even married, should give birth to a baby at all, let alone the Son of God! In Jewish society two thousand years ago, to be an unmarried mother would carry a stigma of shame and disrepute. Not only that, but she and Joseph plainly had very little money or status – the idea of having the baby in a cowshed was something they simply accepted. Could you cope with the challenges that Mary faced at each stage of her journey? I don't think I could.

Sabine Baring-Gould would certainly have been able to identify with some of what Mary and Joseph went through. He had come from quite a well-off family with an estate in Devon, but having chosen the ministry as his life's work, he soon found himself as a young curate in the West Riding of Yorkshire. It was there that his love for life turned to romantic love, because he fell for Grace, the daughter of a millhand, who was then only fourteen years old. The two courted for four years until he finally made her his wife. When Grace died, fifteen children and forty-eight years later, Sabine carved on her tombstone Latin words meaning 'Half my Soul'.

It would have been easy for the people in Mary's town to judge her as soon as her pregnancy became obvious, and to condemn Joseph for standing by her when there was some question about whether or not he was the father. Sabine Baring-Gould was probably aware of similar gossip surrounding his 'inappropriate' affection for a girl who was still only fourteen when he fell in love with her. He and Grace proved all those gossips wrong, though. Their love not only endured, but blossomed into deep devotion over the near half-century they spent together. So much for the gossips!

Baring-Gould was a man who loved children, and who understood that lessons and truths learned in childhood shape the decisions and beliefs of the adult each child would become. As a curate in Horbury Bridge in West Yorkshire, Sabine lived in a tiny cottage where he held a night school downstairs and made a chapel in the bedroom above. Each winter evening, every corner of the house was packed as neighbours poured in to worship, with Sabine balancing on a stool in front of the chimney on which stood a cross and a pair of candlesticks. The crowds also came to learn, because schooling was scarce for most working families then. Children came after a long day's work in the woollen mills, begging him to tell them stories, which he often began with the words every child loves, 'Once upon a time ...' Sabine knew that those stories of Christ's birth, life, death and resurrection told on dark winter evenings were the best chance of providing the young people with a firm foundation for life. For them, it seemed only their ability to work had any value, hardship was rife, their rights non-existent and their opinions irrelevant – a bit like Mary and Joseph, don't you think? The promise and hope of the Christian message gave them the strength to face the many challenges that came their way.

I find myself thinking about Mary and Joseph, and the

trust they had to put in each other as together they faced such a harrowing time. Sabine and Grace had a shaky start to their relationship too, but weathered the storm to share nearly fifty years of Christmases, surrounded by their large and growing family. That's love for you . . .

May this Christmas be the first of many,
Each more joyous in our growing love,
Revealing more of happiness than any
Riches might provide or pain remove.
Years flow like an unrepentant river,
Carrying the soil of life away,
Holding far more than they can deliver,
Rushing past the certitudes that stay.
In love there is an instance of forever
So shy and lovely it eludes the eye,
The sense of being home when we're together,
More enduring than a reason why.
As love is born of passion, borne by will,
So may for many years we choose love still.

(Anonymous)

O come, O come, Emmanuel,
and ransom captive Israel,
that mourns in lonely exile here
until the Son of God appear.

People Get Ready

Chorus: Rejoice! Rejoice!
Emmanuel shall come to thee, O Israel.

O come, thou Wisdom from on high,
who orderest all things mightily;
to us the path of knowledge show,
and teach us in her ways to go.

O come, thou Rod of Jesse, free
thine own from Satan's tyranny;
from depths of hell thy people save,
and give them victory over the grave.

O come, thou Dayspring, come and cheer
our spirits by thine advent here;
disperse the gloomy clouds of night,
and death's dark shadows put to flight.

O come, thou Key of David, come,
and open wide our heavenly home;
make safe the way that leads on high,
and close the path to misery.

O come, O come, great Lord of might,
who to thy tribes on Sinai's height
in ancient times once gave the law
in cloud and majesty and awe.

O come, thou Root of Jesse's tree,
an ensign of thy people be;
before thee rulers silent fall;
all peoples on thy mercy call.

O come, Desire of nations, bind
in one the hearts of all mankind;
bid thou our sad divisions cease,
and be thyself our King of Peace.

O come, O come, Emmanuel,
and ransom captive Israel,
that mourns in lonely exile here
until the Son of God appear.

(Early Latin)

The exact origin of these words stretches back into the mists of time, so it's hard to be precise about exactly when this wonderful summary of the hope, promise and challenge of Christ's coming was written. It's thought that the verses are based on the Latin antiphons sung in the early church for the seven days leading up to Christmas Day, which means they could be as old as the sixth century. However, it wasn't until around the twelfth century that five of those antiphons were put together to produce this hymn. John Henry Newman (the 'Blessed' John Henry Newman, no less, because he was beatified by Pope Benedict at Crofton Park in Birmingham when the Holy Father visited the UK in 2010) translated it into English in 1836, which prompted John Mason Neale, a well-known translator and hymn writer, to put the words to a traditional French melody, thus creating the Advent carol which is now so familiar to us.

Ever since the season of Christmas was established, Christians have treasured Advent as the annual time of preparation for the birth of Christ on earth. Officially, Advent starts on the Sunday nearest to 30 November, and lasts until midnight on Christmas Eve. In churches and homes, candles are lit, cribs dug out and dusted off, Advent calendars bought, gift lists drawn up, addresses updated for Christmas cards, visits planned, houses decorated with lights and garlands and wine cupboards stocked. The lead-up to Christmas Day is full of excitement and anticipation.

> *Christmas is coming,*
> *The goose is getting fat,*
> *Please put a penny in the old man's hat!*
> *If you haven't got a penny, a ha'penny will do,*
> *If you haven't got a ha'penny,*
> *God bless you!*

(Traditional)

If you live in southern Germany the feeling that something special is on its way will be increased by the fact that you're likely to have unpredictable visitors arriving on Klöpfelnächte, 'Knocking Nights', during Advent. Mummer-like figures run from house to house, singing, rapping on doors with rods, throwing pebbles, crying that the Lord is coming and wishing neighbours well.

Or in Bavaria, figures of 'Nikolo-Weibl', a boy dressed as a girl who attends St Nicholas, and twelve 'Buttenmandln', young men in animal masks, skins and cowbells, noisily tramp with St Nicholas from house to house in early Advent. The saint preaches and gifts are given – but then the mood changes as the Buttenmandln try to grab any young people they can catch, and punch them! Apparently that part of the tradition goes back to pre-Christian times and is supposed to bring luck. Not so lucky if all you do is answer the door, but end up with a black eye!

The tradition of electing a boy to become 'St Nicholas's Bishop' was once common in England, France and Germany, but no longer. In cathedrals, choir schools and some parish churches, a choirboy was proclaimed 'bishop' in a ceremony that was sacred, but perhaps a little tongue-in-cheek. The chosen boy was required to wear the full vestments of the genuine bishop from 6 December, St Nicholas's Day, until 28 December, the Day of Holy Innocents. The young 'bishop' was expected to try preaching and performing all of a bishop's usual duties (except mass). If, by any unlikely and unfortunate chance, the 'boy bishop' died while in office, he was buried with full honours. In fact, in Salisbury Cathedral, there is an effigy of a 'boy bishop' who died in just such circumstances. Henry the Eighth wasn't keen on the practice and, with his suppression of the monasteries, the tradition more or less died out in Britain. However, in Europe it continued at least until the eighteenth century.

In Sweden, meanwhile, the Feast of St Lucia is celebrated on 13 December. In times gone by, that day was thought of as the winter solstice, 'the day when the sun stands still', and so that date has always been earmarked as a festival of light.

When monks brought the gospel to Sweden, they told the story of St Lucia, a Christian girl living under the bitter persecution of the Roman Emperor Diocletian. Some legends say that she brought food to Christians in hiding in the catacombs of Rome, wearing lights on her head to leave her hands free. So the pagan festival of light was transformed into the feast of 'St Lucy'.

Traditionally, at the sound of first cock crow, while it is still dark, the youngest daughter of the house (or a young girl chosen by the whole village, church or school), wearing a white robe with a red sash and a wire crown decorated with whortle-berry twigs into which have been placed several lit candles, carries a tray of coffee and saffron buns to each member of the household. She wakes up anyone who's asleep, sings to them, then is proclaimed *Lussi* or *Lussibruden* (Lucy Bride).

In keeping with the idea of the festival of light, breakfast is served in a brightly lit room, and even the family's animals are invited to the feast.

At one time, the day would continue with shooting and fishing by torchlight – and often 'Lussi' visited neighbours' homes, stables, barns and cowsheds, followed by a procession of torchbearers, maids of honour, biblical characters – and a few trolls thrown in for good measure!

In Malta, where I spent many years as a child, it is traditional to sow wheat, grain and canary seed, 'gulbiena', on cotton wool in flat pans five weeks before Christmas. These are left in dark corners in the house until the seeds produce white grass-like shoots. The pans with the fully grown shoots are then used to decorate the crib or the statue of baby Jesus which is sure to be found in every household in this devoutly Catholic island.

And over the Atlantic, on the Caribbean islands of Trinidad and Tobago, they start early with their Christmas prepara-tions. Perhaps it's the round-the-year sunshine that makes everyone on those islands enjoy having parties, but through-out December, whole families go from house to house sharing meals with their neighbours and relatives.

It's the Caribbean custom to paint the house, hang new curtains and make sure everything is repaired, both inside and outside, before the house is covered in fairy lights. There's no waiting for the January sales there! It's *before* Christmas that people choose to buy new electrical appliances and furniture, so that everything is shipshape for the big day.

Trinidad Christmas fruit cake is legendary and a favourite in most homes. You can imagine how delicious the fruits like raisins and sultanas are once they've grown in the sunshine all year round, then been soaked in cherry wine, sherry and rum before the cake is cooked – and then again after!

December the first 'til Christmas
Is the longest time of the year,
It seems as though old Santa
Never will appear.
How many days 'til Christmas?
It's mighty hard to count,
So this little chain of paper
Will show you the exact amount.
Remove one link each day
As the sandman casts his spell,
And Christmas will be here
By the time you reach the bell.

(Anonymous)

One of my earliest memories is of making paper chains at home with my mum. Do you remember doing that too? Mum used to buy little packs of coloured strips of paper which came in several different colours, but all had a glued section at the end which you had to lick, so that you could stick the two ends together to form a circle. Apart from the fact that your mouth tasted horrible and your lips kept sticking together, it was good fun, with each strip fastened around the next until the chains were long enough to string across every room in the house.

Do children still make their own paper chains today? Do they need to when every shop is full of sparkling tinsel in such a range of dazzling colours and thickness? Decorations today are certainly full of variety. I'm the traditional sort who loves garlands and lights to come in the obvious shades of red, green and white – you know, the colours you'd describe as 'jolly'! My husband (he of the snarling top lip and possessive gleam in the eye if anyone goes near his boxes of Christmas lights without permission!) now strings garlands of piercing ice blue lights around the outside of the house, and I have to admit they look very elegant. Not jolly, perhaps – but elegant.

And elegance seems to be the look to aim for these days. You see displays which are all in shades of purple, or pink, silver and turquoise, or gold and black. Elegance somehow passes me by at Christmas, though. Give me old-style gold tinsel (the same strings that have been coming out of our Christmas decorations box for years now!), red baubles, ribbons and the battered old fairy/angel on top, and I couldn't be happier!

Deck the halls with boughs of holly
Fa-la-la-la-la, la-la-la-la

'Tis the season to be jolly
Fa-la-la-la-la, la-la-la-la

Don we now our gay apparel
Fa-la-la, la-la-la, la-la-la.
'Tis the season to be jolly
Fa-la-la-la-la, la-la-la-la.

See the blazing Yule before us.
Fa-la-la-la-la, la-la-la-la
Strike the harp and join the chorus.
Fa-la-la-la-la, la-la-la-la

Follow me in merry measure.
Fa-la-la-la-la, la-la-la-la
While I tell of Yule-tide treasure.
Fa-la-la-la-la, la-la-la-la

Fast away the old year passes.
Fa-la-la-la-la, la-la-la-la
Hail the new, ye lads and lasses
Fa-la-la-la-la, la-la-la-la

Sing we joyous, all together.
Fa-la-la-la-la, la-la-la-la
heedless of the wind and weather.
Fa-la-la-la-la, la-la-la-la

(American, nineteenth century)

No plant is quite so closely associated with Christmas as the holly, with its shining, spiked leaves and bright red berries which, some say, are a symbol of eternal life. This is because of the legend that, beside the stable where Christ was born, a holly tree stood bare of berries, which the birds had eaten. In honour of the new birth, the tree burst into bud, with flowers and berries all in one night. Others claim they represent the drops of blood that fell from Christ's head from the crown of thorns he was made to wear on the cross.

Older generations believe that the holly should only be brought indoors by a man – and as the woman of the household, I love that idea because then *he* can be all manly, and be the one to get his fingers cut to shreds by the thorns and spikes! In days gone by a sprig of holly was nailed up in the cowshed to keep the livestock healthy, and the berries were used as a powerful animal medicine – which was held to be even more powerful if the sprig had come from church decorations. Unlike mistletoe, holly was permitted in churches, along with the softer, clinging ivy, which has a long-time reputation for aiding fertility. Nowadays, almost every church decorates their window ledges and other display areas with bright-berried holly combined with long strands of silvery ivy – and the custom has caught on in our homes as many people try to return to a more traditional style of Christmas decoration with evergreen foliage, branches of pine, and bright red poinsettias – which may have come from sunnier shores, but which have definitely established themselves as a favourite everywhere. In fact, the poinsettia was first discovered in 1834 in Mexico where its Mexican name is 'Flower of the Holy Night' – so it has great pedigree as a Christmas plant!

The Holly and the Ivy

The holly and the ivy,
when they are both full grown,
of all the trees that are in the wood,
the holly bears the crown.

Chorus: O the rising of the sun
and the running of the deer,
the playing of the merry organ,
sweet singing in the choir.

O the holly bears a blossom,
as white as any flower,
and Mary bore sweet Jesus Christ,
to be our sweet Saviour.

O the holly bears a berry,
as red as any blood,
and Mary bore sweet Jesus Christ
to do poor sinners good.

The holly bears a prickle
as sharp as any thorn,
and Mary bore sweet Jesus Christ
on Christmas Day in the morn.

O the holly bears a bark,
as bitter as any gall,
and Mary bore sweet Jesus Christ
for to redeem us all.

The holly and the ivy,
when they are both full grown,
of all the trees that are in the wood,
the holly bears the crown.

(English Folk Carol)

Mistletoe, meanwhile, has always had a formidable reputation for magic wherever it is found, from the Baltic to the Mediterranean. As a parasite that attaches itself to other trees, it grows neither on earth nor in heaven, so is considered to have life-preserving properties. In ancient times, it was revered as a symbol of peace and goodwill. If enemies stood beneath it to speak, the very action of doing so meant they were agreeing a truce until the next day. In some countries, chopping down a mistletoe-bearing tree is still considered to be desecration – and anyone who cuts mistletoe has to make sure it never touches the ground.

Generally, though, the plant is still not welcomed in church – except in York Minster where there was a special ceremony when wrongdoers in the city could come to receive a pardon. The mistletoe used in that ceremony was allowed to stay in the church until Twelfth Night.

Nowadays we hang up mistletoe hoping for a kiss or two under it, following a custom which probably dates back to the Greeks and Romans. The church may have banned the plant but the Victorians (whatever made us think they were strait-laced?) re-introduced mistletoe as an excuse for a kiss! With every kiss a gentleman stole, he had to remove a berry from the plant. Considering how poisonous the berries are, what he must *not* do is to eat any of them. That would certainly cool his passion for kissing . . .

> *Sitting under the mistletoe*
> *One last candle burning low,*
> *All the sleepy dancers gone,*
> *Just one candle burning on,*
> *Shadows lurking everywhere:*
> *Some one came, and kissed me there.*
>
> *Tired I was; my head would go*
> *Nodding under the mistletoe*
> *No footsteps came, no voice, but only,*
> *Just as I sat there, sleepy, lonely,*
> *Stooped in the still and shadowy air*
> *Lips unseen – and kissed me there.*

(Walter de la Mare, 1873–1956)

9

Let Your Little Light Shine

Deep in darkness we begin,
dark outside and deep within.
Now ignite a single flame,
shadows form, let light remain.
Flaming brightly, let love shine,
flaming out through space and time.

As they gleaned the word of life,
narrative of love and strife,
people through each age have known
yet more light: God's glory shown.
Flaming brightly, let love shine,
flaming out through space and time.

Look! a star is shining there
See the stable stark and bare.
Christmas dawns, all darkness gone!
Christ has come, the light shines on!
Flaming brightly, see love shine,
flaming out through space and time.

(Andrew Pratt)

This first hymn text is written by a favourite writer of mine, Andrew Pratt, a Methodist minister who writes poignantly about many aspects of life. Christ is often described as the 'light of the world', which is a powerful image for us during the dark winter days leading up to Christmas. Here Andrew writes about the Advent wreath, on which we light a candle for each Sunday leading up to Christmas.

In churches around the country, those candles become a focus for our prayers, guiding and illuminating our thoughts and actions. There is great comfort in knowing that, even after we've left the church, our prayers will continue to rise to heaven as long as those candle flames burn brightly.

Four Candles

Four candles were burning on the Advent wreath. Everything was so quiet and still that the candles started talking.

The first candle sighed: 'My name is PEACE. My flame is lit but mankind doesn't recognise the value of peace. It seems they just **can't** – or perhaps **won't**.'

And the candle's light got smaller and weaker, then finally went out.

The second candle trembled: 'My name is FAITH, but I feel as if I'm not needed. People don't believe anything any more, unless they can physically touch it and hold it in both hands.'

A breeze of air went through the room and the flickering candle died.

Quietly and timidly, the third candle spoke up: 'My name is LOVE. I no longer have the strength to keep burning. People have become so selfish and uncaring. They only think about what's best for them!'

And with one last flicker, its light also went out.

At that moment, a small boy came into the room. Seeing the candles, he looked puzzled as he said, 'You should be burning! You should **all** be alight. We **need** you!'

Then, the fourth candle spoke. 'Don't be afraid. As long as I'm on fire, I will always be able to give the other candles light and life! My name is HOPE.'

And with a small piece of wood, the boy took the light from the candle of hope, and used it to bring peace, faith and love to life again.

During these dark winter days in the weeks before Christmas, the whole idea of light seems very precious, especially because of the way we use and think of it.

With this Candle

Where there is light,
There is hope.
Where there is friendship –
Peace and truth.
Christmas is a time
For celebrating the special people
in our lives.
When I cannot find my way,
I light a flame.
And at Christmas –
I think of you.

(Anonymous)

Last Christmas I had the moving experience of standing around the Christmas tree in the grounds of our local hospice, along with a crowd of people who were all there because the hospice had cared for someone they'd loved and lost, and had helped family members left behind to cope with their grief. Each glittering candle-shaped light on the tree represented a life lost, a shining celebration of who and how they were, warm with the memory of why they were so valued and cherished. I found it comforting to think that the ones I love and miss so much are still glowing now, no longer in pain – out of our sight, but always in our hearts.

Let Your Little Light Shine

Light a candle,
see it glow,
watch it dance,
when you feel low,
think of me,
think of light,
I'll always be here,
day or night,
a candle flickers,
out of sight,
but in your heart,
I still burn bright,
think not of sadness,
that I'm not near,
think of gladness,
and joyous cheer,
I have not left,
I am not gone,
I'm here to stay
my little one,
so when you light a candle
and you see it glow
and you watch it dance
in your heart you'll know
that I would never leave you
even when you feel so blue
I'm sitting up here with the Lord
and now watching over you.

(Anonymous)

There are other poignant occasions when light makes the moment – like birthdays, when candles celebrate the years of our lives as we blow them out surrounded by our friends and family. There's such joy in those candle flames then, shared and heart-warming. They are in brilliant contrast to the single candle I often light in church. Then, the flickering light represents a prayer – my prayer of thankfulness for all I have, and my plea for God's care and comfort for those around me whom I love, but may be struggling and in pain.

And as Christians light their Advent candles week by week in churches all over the world, we remember how, in Bethlehem two thousand years ago, Christ was born the light of the world. In his light there is all the remembrance, celebration, sharing, care and comfort of God's love – his brilliant, shining blessing on us all.

How far that little candle throws his beams!
So shines a good deed in a weary world.

(William Shakespeare)

A little girl was taken along to church during the Advent season by her mother, who decided they should sit on the front pew so that her daughter could see everything clearly. As the service progressed, the mother tried, as quietly as she could, to explain what was going on.

At one point, robed and very serious, the priest stood close to them, and the girl stared at him. Her mother explained that he was wearing his vestment.

'That's not his vest!' squealed the girl, in that loud, piercing tone all mothers dread. 'That's his nightie!'

Having worked in broadcasting for many years, both on radio and television, I have plenty of experience of the fact that things don't always go quite as planned.

During a recent live radio broadcast for Advent from one of the glorious ancient cathedrals which are such a feature across Britain, the candles of the Advent wreath ended up with a starring role that no one quite expected. The bishop was halfway through his sermon when both he and the congregation noticed that the light of one large candle was flaring up to be several times the size it should be. Apparently, this can happen when a bubble of oxygen gets trapped inside the candle as it's made. Everyone watched in fascination as the flame got higher and higher, with melting wax tumbling down the candle on to the cathedral's much-loved but definitely rather elderly Advent wreath. Eventually, the wreath itself burst into flames while the congregation gasped, the programme makers looked in panic at their watches and the bishop ploughed on with his sermon.

Suddenly, like Superman in a cassock, one of the vergers leapt into action and grabbed a fire extinguisher which had stood unnoticed in a nearby corner for so many years that many wondered if it had been there since the cathedral was first built. After a worrying minute or so while he fumbled with the release mechanism at the top, the verger finally marched purposefully towards the Advent wreath on its stand, and noisily squirted the lot like the hero from an American movie. The programme makers grabbed their earphones in alarm as the noise of the foam being squirted sent the volume dials on their equipment crazy.

And then it was over. The verger stood there staring at the huge blob of foam that had completely covered the Advent wreath, its stand and a wide circle of the floor. The congregation tried hard to resist the temptation to cheer – and the bishop kept talking.

At the end of the live broadcast, having joined the small crowd gathering round the wrecked Advent wreath, the bishop made all the right consoling comments, but secretly found himself thinking that their wreath had been dragged out of a cupboard in the vestry for so many years that it really had been past its best long before its encounter with both candle wax and extinguisher foam! At last, he thought, we can treat ourselves and the cathedral to a new, brightly coloured wreath that looks more pristine and seasonal than the old one. Every cloud has a silver lining!

A week later, he was greeted by the very helpful and charming lady who led the flower-arranging team in the cathedral. With a beaming smile and great flourish, she delved into the large cardboard box she was carrying and pulled out what was unmistakeably the old wreath – with the same old leaves (although no longer coated in candle wax), the same faded colour and the same bald patches in its foliage. It was certainly looking happier than the last time the bishop had seen it, but that wasn't saying much!

'I know how much you love this wreath, bishop!' she enthused. 'So I worked all night to repair it for you. I think it's good for another decade or two, don't you?'

His smile didn't drop even for a moment. Bishops are so well trained these days.

Am I alone in considering computers to be a bit of a mixed blessing? Whenever mine goes wrong (which happens all too often), it's quite humbling to have to find a passing eight-year-old to help me. I think children are born nowadays with more knowledge and natural instinct about computers in their little fingers than I'd ever learn in a lifetime!

Worst of all is the thought of your computer catching a virus, which can do untold damage without you having any idea. Mind you, I rather fancy the idea of catching this one!

The Advent Virus

Anonymous via email

WARNING . . . WARNING: ADVENT VIRUS

Be on the alert for symptoms of inner **Hope, Peace, Joy and Love**. The hearts of a great many have already been exposed to this virus and it is possible that people everywhere could come down with it in epidemic proportions. This could pose a serious threat to what has, up to now, been a fairly stable condition of conflict in the world.

Some signs and symptoms of **The Advent Virus**:

- A tendency to think and act spontaneously rather than based on fears born out of past experiences.

- An unmistakable ability to enjoy each moment.

- A loss of interest in judging other people.

- A loss of interest in interpreting the actions of others.

- A loss of interest in conflict.

- A loss of the ability to worry (this is a very serious symptom).

- Frequent, overwhelming episodes of appreciation.

- Contented feelings of connectedness with others and nature.

- Frequent attacks of smiling.

- An increasing tendency to let things happen rather than make them happen.

- An increased susceptibility to the love extended by others as well as the uncontrollable urge to extend it.

Please send this warning out to all your friends. This virus can and has affected many systems. Some systems have been completely cleaned out because of it.

In September, Matt had passed his driving test, so while Christmas was still some months away he decided to ask his clergyman father if there was any chance of him getting a car as his Christmas present.

His dad listened thoughtfully, then said, 'Look, I'll tell you what I'll do. If you push your predicted A-level grades up to As and Bs, study your Bible a bit more and get your hair cut, I promise I'll give your suggestion proper consideration.'

At the start of December, Matt thought he'd better broach the subject again, so that his dad would have chance to get a car organised.

'Well,' replied his father, 'I have been really impressed by the way you've knuckled down to your A-level work. Your grades are excellent. And it's been good to see how much time you've put into your Bible study too. I have to say, though, that I'm disappointed you've not had your hair cut yet.'

Expecting this reaction, Matt had his answer ready.

'Well,' he began, 'one thing I noticed from the illustrations in my Bible is that Moses, John the Baptist, Samson and even Christ himself had long hair.'

'I am aware of that,' said his father, 'but did you also notice that they walked wherever they went?'

As Christmas gets nearer, I turn my mind to what always feels like the mammoth task of writing Christmas cards. Over the years the family and I seem to have collected something like two hundred people on our card list, and although I've not seen some of them for ages, I still love the thought of keeping in touch, even if it is only once a year.

Some people nowadays jump on the internet instead of sending real Christmas cards, sending round robin messages or little videos of greeting which seem rather impersonal. I find great pleasure, though, in recognising the handwriting of an old friend on an envelope, with the anticipation of catching up on the family news contained inside.

The Spirit of Christmas

I have a list of people I know
All written in a book
And every year at Christmastime
I go and take a look.
And that is when I realise
That those names are a part
Not of the book they're written in
But of my very heart.
For each name stands for someone
Who has crossed my path some time
And in that meeting they've become
A treasured friend of mine.
And once you've met some people
The years cannot erase
The memory of a pleasant word
Or a friendly face.
So when I send a Christmas card
That is addressed to you
It's because you're on that list

Of folk I'm indebted to.
And you are one of many folk who
In times past I've met
And happen to be one of those
I don't want to forget.
And whether I have known you for
Many years or few
In some way you have a part in
Shaping things I do.
This, the spirit of Christmas, that
ever more endures,
May it leave its richest blessing
In the hearts of you and yours.

(Anonymous)

Writing Christmas cards can be a major job, starting with the chore of checking your list to make sure it is up to date with all the most recent address changes. Changes of other sorts need to be taken into account too – like remembering when children have left home, or partnerships have broken up – and new ones begun! Bereavement is the obvious and most moving cause, but there are other situations that can prove a minefield for the most careful of card-senders. Can you imagine the trouble caused when you send a card to a family friend whose wife has left him after many years, and he's moved in a new younger lady! The hardest thing is remembering the right name – it's a minefield of potential upset indeed!

The custom of sending greetings at Christmas goes back a long way – to pagan times in fact, when messages of goodwill at this time of year were often laced with practical good sense.

For example, isolated villages would send seasonal gifts to their neighbours, probably because it was a good idea to be nice to the people who might feed you if supplies ran short!

Before long, the church suppressed the pagan tradition of New Year gifts, along with other ancient practices – but the sending of seasonal greetings re-emerged in the fifteenth century in Germany, when wood-block printing became possible. Cultured, religious Germans would present New Year's gifts called 'Andachtsbilder', which were greetings cards complete with a printed devotional picture for the home. They were often decorated with a scroll and the Christ-child, bearing a cross with the inscription 'Ein gut selig Jahr', meaning 'A good and blessed year.'

Over the following two centuries, such cards grew rare, until the eighteenth century when they began to reappear, but now mostly without any religious words, simply as a seasonal visiting card for friends. If the family you were visiting was away from home, these cards were used to scribble a quick Christmas greeting and left to await their return. They became very popular across Europe, getting more elaborate as time went on. The really affluent would send cards made of silk, while the less well-off might send cards with paper-lace fringes. The Berlin Iron Foundry even sent their customers cards made of cast iron!

At the same time here in Britain, many school children started making a 'Christmas Piece' on coloured paper, which they would take home so that they could show their parents how well their handwriting was coming along. They would add their own loving or rhyming messages on cards that sometimes had an engraved border to add to the coloured decorations they would design themselves.

The start of Christmas greetings cards as we recognise them today is largely due to the first director of London's Victoria and Albert Museum, Sir Henry Cole. For many years, he had been in the habit of sending handwritten greetings to his family and friends on sheets of paper decorated with Christmas themes. Eventually, he decided that this was not very efficient, so he commissioned a Christmas card with a single message that could be duplicated and sent to everyone on his list. The words said, 'A merry Christmas and a happy New Year to you' – a message that has become very familiar down the years ever since!

Sir Henry was definitely a man of action. He went on to play a key role in helping to introduce the Royal Mail's 'Penny Post' service, which meant that suddenly the sending of greetings cards was not just a luxury for the rich but came within the means of many families.

Today, four out of five people say they prefer to receive a card rather than any other form of greeting. After all, lines of cards strung around the walls or on the mantelpiece at Christmas are a cherished part of the decorations that have become traditional in our homes.

And apparently our postmen are responsible for one of the most popular themes on our Christmas cards today. Back in the mid-1800s, the postie's uniform included a bright red waistcoat to match the official red pillar boxes. This led to postmen being nicknamed 'robin redbreasts' – so robins were introduced on Christmas cards as a symbol of the postmen who delivered them.

But today, among all the other familiar Christmas card themes, like snow scenes, roaring fires with stockings hanging from the mantelpiece, Santa Claus and his reindeer, Christmas puddings and ringing bells, the perennial favourites are those which echo the Christmas story – carol singers, a single star, shepherds in the fields, the Magi bearing gifts, Mary and Joseph travelling to Bethlehem, angels in the sky and Christ in the manger.

The First Nowell

The First Nowell the angel did say
Was to certain poor shepherds
in fields as they lay;
In fields as they lay, keeping their sheep,
On a cold winter's night that was so deep.

Chorus: Nowell, Nowell, Nowell, Nowell,
Born is the King of Israel.

They looked up and saw a star
Shining in the east beyond them far,
And to the earth it gave great light,
And so it continued both day and night.

And by the light of that same star
Three wise men came from country far;
To seek for a king was their intent,
And to follow the star wherever it went.

This star drew nigh to the northwest,
O'er Bethlehem it took its rest,
And there it did both stop and stay
Right over the place where Jesus lay.

Let Your Little Light Shine

Then entered in those wise men three
Full reverently upon their knee,
and offered there in his presence
Their gold, and myrrh, and frankincense.

Then let us all with one accord
Sing praises to our heavenly Lord;
That hath made heaven and earth of naught,
And with his blood mankind hath bought

(Traditional)

Mary's Song

And Mary said:
'My soul glorifies the Lord
and my spirit rejoices in God my Saviour,
for he has been mindful
of the humble state of his servant.
From now on all generations will call me blessed,
for the Mighty One has done great things for me –
holy is his name.
His mercy extends to those who fear him,
from generation to generation.
He has performed mighty deeds with his arm;
he has scattered those who are proud in their inmost
thoughts.
He has brought down rulers from their thrones
but has lifted up the humble.
He has filled the hungry with good things
but has sent the rich away empty.'

(Luke 1:46-53)

10

Prayers and Presents

Tell Out, My Soul, the Greatness of the Lord

*Based on the New English Bible translation of the
Magnificat, Luke 1:46-55*

Tell out, my soul, the greatness of the Lord!
Unnumbered blessings, give my spirit voice;
tender to me the promise of his word;
in God my Saviour shall my heart rejoice.

Tell out, my soul, the greatness of his Name!
Make known his might, the deeds his arm has done;
his mercy sure, from age to age the same;
his holy Name, the Lord, the Mighty One.

Tell out, my soul, the greatness of his might!
Powers and dominions lay their glory by.
Proud hearts and stubborn wills are put to flight,
the hungry fed, the humble lifted high.

Tell out, my soul, the glories of his word!
Firm is his promise, and his mercy sure.

Tell out, my soul, the greatness of the Lord
to children's children and for evermore!

(Timothy Dudley-Smith)

Ever the wordsmith, Bishop Timothy Dudley-Smith is one of my favourite hymn-writers, present or past. Now in his late eighties, with one of the liveliest and most creative minds I've ever come across, he writes about every aspect of the Christian life in a way that challenges, comforts and inspires. The hymn above was one of his first, written way back in 1962, and yet it has the classic feel of a traditional hymn of praise. The simplicity and sincerity of his paraphrasing of 'Mary's Song' have made these words almost as familiar as the original!

Can there be anything to melt your heart more than the sight of small children acting out the nativity story? If you're a parent, absolutely not. If you're the children's teacher, you may need the patience of a saint!

The Nativity Play

Oh Miss, I don't want to be Joseph,
Miss, I really don't want to be him.
With a cloak of bright red and a towel on my head
And a cotton-wool beard on my chin.

Prayers and Presents

Oh Miss, please don't make me a shepherd.
I just won't be able to sleep.
I'll go weak at the knees – and wool makes me sneeze
And I really am frightened of sheep.

Oh Miss, I just can't be the landlord
Who says there's no room at the inn.
I'll get in a fright when it comes to the night
And I know that I'll let Mary in.

Oh Miss, you're not serious – an angel?
Can't Peter take that part instead?
I'll look such a clown in a white silky gown,
And a halo stuck up on my head.

Oh Miss, I'm not being a camel –
Or a cow or an ox or an ass!
I'll look quite absurd and I won't say a word,
But still all the audience will laugh.

Oh Miss, I'd rather not be a Wise Man
Who brings precious gifts from afar.
But the part right for me – and I hope you'll agree –
In this play – Can't I Just Be THE STAR?

(Gervase Phinn)

One of my favourite memories is of my son, Max, when he was just five years old, being chosen for the great honour of playing Joseph in the school nativity play.

I sat in the front row holding my breath as he gently led Mary (who was about three inches taller than him) across the stage, where they stopped in front of the inn door. As he knocked, the whole structure shook alarmingly, threatening to fall over completely as a very grumpy-looking five-year-old innkeeper stepped out to meet them.

'My wife and I have travelled so far and we are very tired,' said Joseph. 'Is there any room at the inn?'

'No!' said the innkeeper. 'Go away!'

'But my wife is about to have a baby,' pleaded Joseph. 'Isn't there anywhere at all that you could squeeze us in?'

'No!' snapped the innkeeper. 'Push off!'

By this time, Joseph was getting desperate.

'Look,' he insisted, 'we have got to stay here . . .'

'Oh no, you haven't,' sobbed the innkeeper. 'I wanted to be Joseph . . .!'

Advent 1955

> *The Advent wind begins to stir*
> *With sea-like sounds in our Scotch fir,*
> *It's dark at breakfast, dark at tea,*
> *And in between we only see*
> *Clouds hurrying across the sky*

And rain-wet roads the wind blows dry
And branches bending to the gale
Against great skies all silver-pale.
The world seems travelling into space,
And travelling at a faster pace
Than in the leisured summer weather
When we and it sit out together,
For now we feel the world spin round
On some momentous journey bound –
Journey to what? to whom? to where?
The Advent bells call out 'Prepare,
Your world is journeying to the birth
Of God made Man for us on earth.'

And how, in fact, do we prepare
The great day that waits us there –
The twenty-fifth day of December,
The birth of Christ? For some it means
An interchange of hunting scenes
On coloured cards. And I remember
Last year I sent out twenty yards,
Laid end to end, of Christmas cards
To people that I scarcely know –
They'd sent a card to me, and so
I had to send one back. Oh dear!
Is this a form of Christmas cheer?
Or is it, which is less surprising,
My pride gone in for advertising?
The only cards that really count
Are that extremely small amount
From real friends who keep in touch

And are not rich but love us much
Some ways indeed are very odd
By which we hail the birth of God.

We raise the price of things in shops,
We give plain boxes fancy tops
And lines which traders cannot sell
Thus parcell'd go extremely well.
We dole out bribes we call a present
To those to whom we must be pleasant
For business reasons. Our defence is
These bribes are charged against expenses
And bring relief in Income Tax
Enough of these unworthy cracks!
'The time draws near the birth of Christ',
A present that cannot be priced
Given two thousand years ago.
Yet if God had not given so
He still would be a distant stranger
And not the Baby in the manger.

(John Betjeman, 1906–84)

I so enjoy John Betjeman's spiky style of writing, combining his artistry as a poet with his keen eye for detail in the world around him. He wrote this remembering his feelings about the lead-up to Christmas in 1955 – but I can't help feeling that his sentiments ring even truer today, especially in the last two verses. There is an unsettling commercialism to Christmas that puts pressure on all of us to overspend, tempted by advertising to buy items that we don't really need to fuel our celebrations, as well as spending lavishly on presents for others that we may be giving out of a sense of duty and habit as much as love.

The lines that stand out most for me are towards the end. Among all the frantic build-up to Christmas, as we panic about what we need and what we haven't got, this is the simple truth at the very heart of everything:

> *'The time draws near the birth of Christ',*
> *A present that cannot be priced*

A few days before Christmas, two young brothers were spending the night at their grandparents' house. Knowing how their grandmother liked to know they were dutiful in saying their prayers, when it was time to go to bed they both knelt down, put their hands together and bowed their heads.

Suddenly the younger boy began to speak in a very loud voice.

'Dear God, please ask Santa Claus to bring me a remote control racing car and a mountain bike. Thank you!'

The bigger boy leaned over and nudged him.

'Why are you shouting? God isn't deaf.'

'I know,' grinned his brother, 'but Grandma is!'

A Letter to St Nick

Dear Father Christmas, please be kind
And leave me lots of stuff behind.

I'd like a bike but I won't fret
If all I get's a painting set.

It's all the rest that live here too
That need some bits and bobs from you.

Like Dad, who says he likes Old Spice,
Please! CK One is twice as nice!

For Mum, whose nails are varnished red,
Please send her some pale pink instead.

My brother has a room that stinks
Although it's trendy (so he thinks)
To wear the same clothes every day.
Send LYNX to take the smell away.

My sister, the last of the really big spenders,
Loves that young guy off EASTENDERS.
Send her his poster, Santa, do –
And one for me – I like him too!

Here's just two more who need a treat
Although they're old with aching feet;
Gran and Grandad end my list.

By now I think you've got the gist.
Send Granny chocolates – she's on a diet.
Grandad? He just wants peace and quiet.

Whatever else the season brings,
I hope that YOU get some nice things.
'Cos just like socks don't make Dad merry,
You must be really sick of sherry!

(Alan Titchmarsh)

I think if it weren't for mums, a lot of the traditions of Christmas just wouldn't happen – or is it only me who feels like Santa's Little Elf as the Big Day looms? I find myself not only wrapping presents for all the friends and family, but also quite a lot of gifts which I choose, buy and the wrap for one member of the family to give to another, because they say they can't quite manage to get around to it themselves! It is hard work, but I have to admit I love it all.

Correction, I'm going to qualify that. I love it all except for the occasions when I try to encourage my husband, Richard, to come along and choose some of the Christmas gifts with me – in other words, to go shopping! When we were courting, Richard used to say he loved shopping. Ever since we've been married, he may eventually agree to come along, but once we're at the shops, he can be infuriatingly reluctant to enter into the spirit of the thing.

Last Christmas, we went into our local shopping arcade to do our main Christmas gift shopping. After about an hour, while I was waiting to pay in a particularly long queue, I turned round and found he'd disappeared! A quarter of an hour of searching later, there was still no sign of him – so, in exasperation, I rang him.

'Where are you?' I asked when he finally answered.

'You remember when we used to come to this arcade before we were married,' he asked, 'and we found that lovely little jeweller's shop on the corner just outside?'

'Yes,' was my curt reply.

'And when we looked in the window, you saw those eternity rings with all the diamonds, and said how much you liked them?'

'Yes,' I replied slowly, curious now about where this was going.

'And we decided that we couldn't afford one now, but in the future, if ever we had enough money, I would buy one of those eternity rings for you?'

'Yes . . .!' I couldn't hide the anticipation in my voice.

'Well, I'm in the cafe next door having a bacon butty. I'm starving!'

Shopping in December, a man saw a fantastic train set. 'I'll take it,' he told the assistant.

'I'm sure your son will love it,' said the assistant.

'You're probably right,' said the man. 'I'd better have two.'

Another nativity play, another town, this time in the heart of rural England. The three Wise Men appear from the side of the stage, grandly dressed in shiny tunics of red and gold, with jewelled crowns on their heads. They are each carrying a precious gift – which, it has to be said, all look a bit like coffee jars covered in tin foil, which is exactly what they are!

The tallest Wise Man has the responsibility of speaking on behalf of them all. He takes centre stage, pulling himself up to his full height as he tells the audience: 'We are Three Kings who have travelled from the East following a star. We have come to find the newborn child, and we bear precious gifts of gold, frankincense – and manure!'

❇

When I finally get as far as wrapping some of the presents I've bought for people I love at Christmas, I keep catching myself wrapping one thing, but wishing I could actually give them another – a gift that would never fit into Christmas paper!

For example, there I was wrapping up the latest bestselling novel for a young man who's got far too much time to read these days because he was made redundant three months ago. Although he's well qualified and has applied for dozens of jobs, in that time there's been no prospect of any proper employment at all. That's dented his pride, undermined his confidence and left him feeling really worthless. So the present I'd love to be able to give him this year is one of the great gifts of Christmas – hope; a hope that he never loses sight of how unique and wonderful he is – or his belief that, because of everything he is, eventually things will work out for him.

And then, I was wrapping a lovely book of tea-time recipes for an elderly lady who's loved baking all her life. Not so much now, though. She told me a while back that she sometimes wonders why she bothers getting up each morning when she spends most days alone and in pain. How dearly I'd love to give her the gift of faith – faith that, even though she lives alone, she is valued by those who love her, and that, because of the child born in a stable two thousand years ago, she is never alone, and that God is just a prayer away, reassuring and comforting.

Finally, there are the two middle-aged sisters who'd always been close, until they argued years ago, and haven't spoken to each other since. As I wrap their identical parcels of bath-time goodies, I wish so much that I could give each of them the gifts of tolerance and forgiveness. Carrying a sense of injustice and resentment inside them all this time has hurt not just them, but those around them who love both. I'd so like to see them let go of that burden and leave it in the past so they can rediscover the good in each other again.

I suppose I really wish I could enclose between the layers of paper on every present I wrap the love I feel for them all, a love which is only a pale reflection of what I know to be the greatest blessing of all – God's love that came down to us at Christmas.

O little town of Bethlehem, how still we see thee lie!
Above thy deep and dreamless sleep the silent stars go
*   by.*
Yet in thy dark streets shineth the everlasting Light;
The hopes and fears of all the years are met in thee
*   tonight.*

For Christ is born of Mary, and gathered all above,
While mortals sleep, the angels keep their watch of
*   wondering love.*
O morning stars together, proclaim the holy birth,
And praises sing to God the King, and peace to men on
*   earth!*

How silently, how silently, the wondrous Gift is
*   giv'n;*
So God imparts to human hearts the blessings of His
*   Heav'n.*
No ear may hear His coming, but in this world of sin,
Where meek souls will receive Him still, the dear Christ
*   enters in.*

Where children pure and happy pray to the blessèd
*   Child,*
Where misery cries out to Thee, Son of the mother
*   mild;*
Where charity stands watching and faith holds wide the
*   door,*
The dark night wakes, the glory breaks, and Christmas
*   comes once more.*

O holy Child of Bethlehem, descend to us, we pray;
Cast out our sin, and enter in, be born in us today.
We hear the Christmas angels the great glad tidings tell;
O come to us, abide with us, our Lord Emmanuel!

(Phillips Brooks, 1835–93)

The Birth of John the Baptist

When it was time for Elizabeth to have her baby, she gave birth to a son. Her neighbours and relatives heard that the Lord had shown her great mercy, and they shared her joy.

On the eighth day they came to circumcise the child, and they were going to name him after his father Zechariah, but his mother spoke up and said, 'No! He is to be called John.'

They said to her, 'There is no one among your relatives who has that name.'

Then they made signs to his father, to find out what he would like to name the child. He asked for a writing tablet, and to everyone's astonishment he wrote, 'His name is John.' Immediately his mouth was opened and his tongue set free, and he began to speak, praising God. All the neighbours were filled with awe, and throughout the hill country of Judea people were talking about all these things. Everyone who heard this wondered about it, asking, 'What then is this child going to be?' For the Lord's hand was with him.

(Luke 1:57-66)

II

Laughter and Tears

Away in a manger, no crib for a bed,
The little Lord Jesus laid down His sweet head.
The stars in the sky looked down where He lay,
The little Lord Jesus, asleep on the hay.

The cattle are lowing, the Baby awakes,
But little Lord Jesus, no crying He makes;
I love Thee, Lord Jesus, look down from the sky
And stay by my side until morning is nigh.

Be near me, Lord Jesus, I ask Thee to stay
Close by me forever, and love me, I pray;
Bless all the dear children in Thy tender care,
And fit us for Heaven to live with Thee there.

(Unknown)

To be a teacher in a junior school in the days leading up to Christmas takes a very special kind of person. Faced with an over-excited class of youngsters, all buzzing with anticipation as Christmas looms nearer, requires the ability to organise with military precision, the patience of a saint, a sense of proportion, a tendency to laugh whenever you can (especially at yourself!), a ready supply of soothing, encouraging words – and the ability to survive on very little sleep. Christmas plays, school parties and outings, tearful children, demanding parents – all challenging, fulfilling, exhausting, tremendous fun!

I bet those teachers are more than ready for the school holidays . . .

'Twas the Daze Before Christmas

'Twas the daze before Christmas,
And all through the school,
The teachers were trying
To just keep their cool.

The hallways were hung
With Christmas art
(Some made in November
to get a head start!)

The children were bouncing
Off ceilings and walls,
And seemed to forget
How to walk in the halls.

When out of the teacher's lounge
With 'holiday shirts' and 'jingle bell jewels',
The teachers looked festive
Enforcing the rules.

Suddenly, from down the hallway
There came such a chatter,
The principal went in
To see what was the matter.

The teachers were hiding
And trying to refuel,
On coffee and cookies
And treats from the Yule.

When what to their wondering
Ears do they hear,
But the ringing of school bells –
It's the children they fear!

More rapid than reindeer
The little ones came,
And the teachers all shouted
And called them by name;

Walk, Vincent! Walk, Tanner!
Walk, Tyler and Sammy!
Sit, Jamie! Sit, Laura!
Sit, Tara and Tammy!

To your desks in the room!
To your spots in the line!
Now walk to them! Walk to them!
No running this time!

So straight to their places
The children all went.
With fear of detention
Where they could be sent.

With manuals of lessons
Cradled in arms,
The teachers began
To use all their charms.

But the lessons presented
All fell on deaf ears.
The children were thinking
Of Santa's reindeer!

With a toss of their hands
They put manuals aside,
Went straight to the cupboards
Where videos hide.

And laying their finger
On the TV remote
They sat back to write
Their last Christmas note.

But you could hear them exclaim
At the end of the day –
Have a wonderful, happy and
L-O-O-O-O-O-NG HOLIDAY!!!

(Anonymous)

The Advent play had been going really well, until the Three Kings arrived from the East, and a very unholy scuffle broke out. One lad stuck his hand up in the air and, with tears in his eyes, wailed, 'Miss, Miss, he hit me with his Frankenstein!'

Three things are required at Christmas time,
Plum pudding, beef and pantomime.
Folks could resist the former two;
Without the latter none could do!

(Anonymous)

This rhyme was a strapline on an old pantomime playbill – and whoever wrote it would probably be very pleased to know that, even now that we're well into the twenty-first century, we British love our pantomimes more than ever!

It helps if you have the excuse of children, or even grandchildren, whom you just *have* to take along to your local theatre, where *Sleeping Beauty, Aladdin, Cinderella, Snow White and the Seven Dwarfs* or some other classic fairy story is being performed in inimitable pantomime style. Nowadays, though, pantomimes are so popular that adults often just go along because they love them! Sparkling sets, worried villagers, the hapless 'down-on-her-luck' mother (often a man dressed up as a woman) with her handsome son (often a woman dressed up as a man – are you keeping up?), the beautiful princess, the wicked wizard, an Ugly Sister or two, the pot of gold in a deep dark cave, the 'all together now' choruses, gorgeous costumes and the happy-ever-after ending – we love them! Pantomimes have become as much a part of the tradition of Christmas across Britain as Santa himself.

Oh yes they are! Oh no they're not!

Panto!

Ladies and gentlemen, girls and boys,
We thank you for coming along,
You're in for a very special night,
Of laughter, dance and song.

The plot is very loosely based,
On a story that you know,
Updated with a modern twist,
And gags throughout the show.

Some of the girls are dressed as boys,
And some of the guys are dames,

And beneath those silly wigs you'll spot
Some very famous names . . .

The stage is set for custard pies,
And lots of messy fun,
Flashes, bangs and puffs of smoke,
And glitter by the ton.

The script is very cheeky,
And rather blue in style,
With plenty of double meanings,
To make the grown-ups smile.

We're counting on the kiddies,
And all the dads and mums,
To shout out when they're told to,
And boo when the villain comes.

Well, that is quite enough from me,
There's nothing more to say.
So let us raise the curtain now,
And start our little play.

We hope it doesn't bore you
(We're pretty sure it won't)
But if we catch you sneaking out.
We'll shout 'OH NO YOU DON'T!'

(Higgs)

When it comes to the stories we enjoy more than ever at Christmas time, there is no writer more loved by generations of children than Hans Christian Andersen. He was born in the town of Odense in Denmark in 1805, and by the time he was eleven, his father had died, leaving him in the care of his mother, who was dismally poor, uneducated and working as a washer-woman. Hans, though, had an outstanding soprano voice, and at the age of fourteen he moved to Copenhagen seeking work as an actor. He was taken on by the Royal Danish Theatre – but then when his voice broke, he began to focus on writing down some of the wonderful stories that filled his head. Unforgettable tales like 'The Princess and the Pea', 'Thumbelina', 'The Little Mermaid' and 'The Emperor's New Clothes' followed, and his fame spread so far that eventually he travelled to England where he struck up a friendship with Charles Dickens.

The two shared something in common as writers. They understood the plight of those who lived in abject poverty – and they wove something of the reality and the spirit of desperately poor people into their stories, along with an element of campaigning for justice and fairness for all.

There can be few stories that touch the conscience with quite as much pathos as that classic Christmas story of 'The Little Match Girl'.

The Little Match Girl

It was terribly cold and nearly dark on the last evening of the old year, and the snow was falling fast. In the cold and the darkness, a poor little girl, with bare head and naked feet, roamed through the streets. It is true she had on a pair of slippers when she left home, but they were not of much use. They were very large, so large, indeed, that they had belonged to her mother, and the poor little creature had lost them in running across the street to avoid two carriages that were rolling along at a terrible rate. One of the slippers she could not find, and a boy seized upon the other and ran away with it, saying that he could use it as a cradle, when he had children of his own.

So the little girl went on with her little naked feet, which were quite red and blue with the cold. In an old apron she carried a number of matches, and had a bundle of them in her hands. No one had bought anything of her the whole day, nor had anyone given her even a penny. Shivering with cold and hunger, she crept along; poor little child, she looked the picture of misery. The snowflakes fell on her long, fair hair, which hung in curls on her shoulders, but she regarded them not.

Lights were shining from every window, and there was a savoury smell of roast goose, for it was New-year's eve – yes, she remembered that. In a corner, between two houses, one of which projected beyond the other, she sank down and huddled herself together. She had drawn her little feet under her, but she could not keep off the cold; and she dared not go home, for she had sold no matches, and could not take home even a penny of money. Her father would certainly beat her; besides, it was almost as cold at home as here, for they had only the roof to cover them, through which the wind howled, although the largest holes had been stopped up with straw and rags. Her little hands were almost frozen with the cold.

Ah! perhaps a burning match might be some good, if she could draw it from the bundle and strike it against the wall, just to warm her fingers. She drew one out – 'scratch!' how it sputtered as it burnt! It gave a warm, bright light, like a little candle, as she held her hand over it. It was really a wonderful light. It seemed to the little girl that she was sitting by a large iron stove, with polished brass feet and a brass ornament. How the fire burned! and seemed so beautifully warm that the child stretched out her feet as if to warm them, when, lo! the flame of the match went out, the stove vanished, and she had only the remains of the half-burnt match in her hand.

She rubbed another match on the wall. It burst into a flame, and where its light fell upon the wall it became as transparent as a veil, and she could see into the room. The table was covered with a snowy white table-cloth, on which stood a splendid dinner service, and a steaming roast goose, stuffed with apples and dried plums. And what was still more wonderful, the goose jumped down from the dish and waddled across the floor, with a knife and fork in its breast, to the little girl. Then the match went out, and there remained nothing but the thick, damp, cold wall before her.

She lighted another match, and then she found herself sitting under a beautiful Christmas-tree. It was larger and more beautifully decorated than the one which she had seen through the glass door at the rich merchant's. Thousands of tapers were burning upon the green branches, and coloured pictures, like those she had seen in the show-windows, looked down upon it all. The little one stretched out her hand towards them, and the match went out.

The Christmas lights rose higher and higher, till they looked to her like the stars in the sky. Then she saw a star fall, leaving behind it a bright streak of fire. 'Someone is dying,' thought the little girl, for her old grandmother, the only one who had ever loved her, and who was now dead, had told her that when a star falls, a soul was going up to God.

She again rubbed a match on the wall, and the light shone round her; in the brightness stood her old grandmother, clear and shining, yet mild and loving in her appearance. 'Grandmother,' cried the little one, 'O take me with you; I know you will go away when the match burns out; you will vanish like the warm stove, the roast goose, and the large, glorious Christmas-tree.' And she made haste to light the whole bundle of matches, for she wished to keep her grandmother there. And the matches glowed with a light that was brighter than the noon-day, and her grandmother had never appeared so large or so beautiful. She took the little girl in her arms, and they both flew upwards in brightness and joy far above the earth, where there was neither cold nor hunger nor pain, for they were with God.

In the dawn of morning there lay the poor little one, with pale cheeks and smiling mouth, leaning against the wall; she had been frozen to death on the last evening of the year; and the New-year's sun rose and shone upon a little corpse! The child still sat, in the stiffness of death, holding the matches in her hand, one bundle of which was burnt. 'She tried to warm herself,' said some. No one imagined what beautiful things she had seen, nor into what glory she had entered with her grandmother, on New-year's day.

(Hans Christian Andersen 1805–75)

Over the years, St Thomas, thought of as 'Doubting Thomas' within the circle of Christ's apostles, has been made the patron saint of old people and children. On his saint's day on 21 December, old and young people alike were traditionally allowed to go round collecting money to buy food for their Christmas dinners. The custom was called a-Thomasing, or sometimes a-mumping or a-gooding!

The children would present a sprig of holly or mistletoe to anyone kind enough to put money their box. And back in 1785, Parson James Woodforde wrote in his diary: 'This being St Thomas' Day, had a great many Poor People of the Parish to visit me. I gave to each of them that came, sixpence.'

Nowadays, that tradition of offering practical help to people in need is at the heart of the Christingle services which are becoming more and more popular in churches across the UK. The idea of Christingle began in the Moravian congregation of Marienborn in Germany on 20 December, 1747. Minister John de Watteville held a children's service in which he explained that happiness had come to people through Jesus 'who has kindled in each little heart a flame which keeps burning to their joy and our happiness.' To make the point clear, each child then received a little lighted wax candle, tied round with a red ribbon. The minister ended the service with this prayer: 'Lord Jesus, kindle a flame in these children's hearts, that theirs like Thine will become.'

The minister then ended his diary entry about the service with the words: 'Hereupon the children went full of joy with their lighted candles to their rooms and so went glad and happy to bed.'

Over the last fifty years, the custom of the Christingle has been revived, and often the candlelit services encourage congregations to be aware of the needs of children, families and the homeless, with a retiring collection held for a chosen local charity.

Children are each given a 'Christingle', traditionally an orange, representing the world, with a lit candle representing Christ, the light of the world. Nuts, raisins and sweets on cocktail sticks around the candle represent God's bounty and goodness in providing the fruits of the earth – and red paper in a frill around the base of the candle or a ribbon around the orange reminds us of the blood of Christ shed for all on the cross.

Remember Them

We open our presents, laugh together, sit down to eat. But beyond the window – out there in the darkness – are those for whom Christmas brings no respite. For them it is another day of loneliness, fear, imprisonment, hunger, sickness, homelessness, weariness and war.

To many, even a shabby bedsitter would be a splendid place – dry, warm, safe and large enough to house a family. To many our full larders, our clean water, our health, our peace of mind, our united families are things of which they can only dream. Some knew our world once – and have lost it, or been exiled from it, or had it taken from them. Some have never known anything but fear and poverty and loss. It is right to show our love for one another at Christmas – to share a meal, to exchange gifts, to be happy.

But I wish that we privileged few could hear the voices of all those beyond our windows.

If only now, at Christmas, we could bring them in, share our thoughts and hear their individual stories. For they are not statistics, international problems, drains on government resources.

They are individuals, each complex and unique.

Valuable. As we are.

(Pam Brown)

Christ told us we should love one another, and with his actions and parables like 'The Good Samaritan' he made clear how widely we should apply that – and yet we are mostly inclined to care for those who are within our own circle. Christ told us to love our neighbour – but in a world that grows ever smaller through communication and high-speed travel, our neighbours could be anywhere on the globe.

John Greenleaf Whittier, the American Quaker poet who wrote the words of the much-loved hymn 'Dear Lord and Father of mankind', throws out a challenge to us all as Christmas approaches:

The Joy You Give

Somehow, not only for Christmas
But all the long year through,
The joy that you give to others
Is the joy that comes back to you.
And the more you spend in blessing
The poor and lonely and sad,
The more of your heart's possessing
Returns to you glad.

(John Greenleaf Whittier, 1807–92)

The Birth of Jesus

In those days Caesar Augustus issued a decree that a census should be taken of the entire Roman world. (This was the first census that took place while Quirinius was governor of Syria.) And everyone went to their own town to register.

So Joseph also went up from the town of Nazareth in Galilee to Judea, to Bethlehem the town of David, because he belonged to the house and line of David. He went there to register with Mary, who was pledged to be married to him and was expecting a child. While they were there, the time came for the baby to be born, and she gave birth to her firstborn, a son. She wrapped him in cloths and placed him in a manger, because there was no guest room available for them.

(Luke 2:1-7)

12

Christmas Eve

Oh, holy night, the stars are brightly shining;
It is the night of the dear Saviour's birth!
Long lay the world in sin and error pining,
Till He appeared and the soul felt its worth.
A thrill of hope, the weary soul rejoices,
For yonder breaks a new and glorious morn.
Fall on your knees, oh, hear the angel voices!
Oh, night divine, oh, night when Christ was born!
Oh, night divine, oh, night, oh, night divine!

Truly He taught us to love one another;
His law is love and His Gospel is peace.
Chains shall He break for the slave is our brother,
And in His Name all oppression shall cease.
Sweet hymns of joy in grateful chorus raise we,
Let all within us praise His holy Name!
Christ is the Lord! Oh, praise His name forever!
His pow'r and glory evermore proclaim!
His pow'r and glory evermore proclaim!

(Placide Cappeau, 1808–1877, translated and
adapted by John Sullivan Dwight, 1813–1893)

For Christmas Eve, the day that leads up to the most wonderful night of the year, I have chosen a carol which is, without doubt, one of the most beautiful ever written. It's rarely sung by congregations, and yet for the past few years, 'O holy night' has been chosen by *Songs of Praise* viewers as their favourite of all carols. The melody is soaring and tuneful, the words touching and evocative. They were written just before Christmas in 1847 in the little town of Roquemaure, near Avignon, France. The writer was none other than the mayor of the town, Placide Cappeau, who combined his mayoral duties with a love of writing poetry. Sensing that this particular text was one of his best yet, he went to Paris to meet up with his composer friend Charles Adolphe Adam. The result of their combined talent was this glorious carol, which was sung for the first time at midnight mass in Roquemaure on Christmas Eve that year.

What a beautiful carol to be singing in your heart as Christmas Eve dawns with all the excitement of the day ahead. As last-minute preparations are organised and family and friends gather, it's easy to forget what prompted it all that first Christmas in Bethlehem two thousand years ago – a couple travelling far away from home, on a journey made all the more difficult because the young woman was about to have her first baby. What made matters worse was that there seemed to be nowhere they could stay. Everywhere was full. How was that young woman feeling, I wonder – and what about the man travelling at her side? What thoughts had filled his mind over the previous weeks and months as events unfolded, and the time for both their journey and the birth of the baby grew closer?

Joe

Joseph sat back in his workshop chair and stared ahead, only he wasn't really looking at anything.

Yesterday his mind had been on how he could arrange the journey to Bethlehem – because he had to be registered there for taxation purposes. He knew this was important and that whether he agreed with the Roman occupation or not, he would have to go to Bethlehem because his family had come from the line of David. In fact, he had been born there.

Not far from his thoughts too, for the last few months, had been the approaching wedding day, the day he married his lovely Mary and after which he could be with his young bride all the time. She was such a catch – beautiful, generous, patient and full of hope and integrity. It was such a special relationship. He wanted to share his life with her, for ever.

Now, a shattered dream.

A lot had happened recently. Mary had been away, staying with her cousin who was expecting a baby, a child she never thought she would be able to have. But now Mary was pregnant – his girl, pregnant and he was not responsible. She had told him something about God being involved! She'd seemed so sure. His heart seemed ripped apart.

'Hey, we have a contract!' he'd exclaimed to himself.

'She – she belongs to me, not to another. I really loved her . . . but this does not happen to good Jewish girls . . . or men. We will be disgraced, her especially . . . I'll have to get some witnesses and divorce her quietly somewhere and soon.'

Betrayal, though, was his strongest sense. Betrayal, sadness and burgeoning bitterness, in both his heart and his head.

Pregnancy out of wedlock is dirty, unworthy, indecent. This is how it had been from ancient times; morality that had often set Israel apart from other nations. It was ingrained into Joseph. No, divorce it must be.

But then, THE DREAM. He breathed deeply. He was awake. He was thinking clearly. THE ANGEL. People had always searched for God, but would God search for men in this way?

He drew his clasped hands away from the back of his scalp. A dream. A vivid dream. A dream so real he could remember everything about it – the brightness, the compelling voice, his own manner, his racing heart-beat . . . Just a few moments ago his thinking, his heart, his world had been turned upside-down. What had happened? These words:

'Joseph, son of David, do not be afraid to take Mary as your wife, for the child conceived in her is from the Holy Spirit. She will bear a son, and you are to name him Jesus, for he will save his people from their sins.'

He hardly needed to process what he'd heard. 'Could this really be the fulfilment of the ancient story? That of the Messiah? Do I matter in all this? Does God want me to marry Mary? Can we be together as we'd planned?'

Yes, Joseph thought. He mattered. He mattered to God. He was to be part of an amazing plan.

He was shaking. Shaking with joy, with shock, with love.

He could hang on in there. He could do more than that. They could marry, they could travel to Bethlehem together, but he would have a pregnant wife to take care of. He felt the awesomeness of the responsibility but also the presence of God. God – who had sent His angel to him, Joseph!

Who would believe him? . . . Mary would!

'Mary! Mary!' he cried aloud. Whipping off his apron, he tore out of the door, turned left down the path, a path he'd dreaded walking just a few hours earlier. Now he couldn't wait to see her again, to tell her it was going to be alright. Incredible and yet credible! A special relationship. Cosmic, in fact!

(Hilary Jane Hughes)

In churches and schools up and down the country, children act out the events of that first Christmas Eve. This is a popular story about a strange procession of visitors – and one very grumpy innkeeper.

Jesus' Christmas Party

There was nothing the innkeeper liked more than a good night's sleep – but that night there was a knock at the door.

'No room,' said the innkeeper.

'But we're tired and have travelled through night and day.'

'Well, there's only the STABLE round the back. Here's two blankets. Sign the register.'

So they signed it, 'MARY AND JOSEPH'.

Then he shut the door, climbed the stairs, got into bed and went to sleep.

But then, later, there was another knock at the door.

'Excuse me, I wonder if you could lend us another SMALLER blanket?'

'There. One smaller blanket,' said the innkeeper.

Then he shut the door, climbed the stairs, got into bed, and went to sleep.

But then a bright light woke him up.

'That's ALL I need!' said the innkeeper.

So he went downstairs again and was dazzled by the brightness of a star in the sky shining right down on his inn. He slammed the door shut, climbed the stairs, drew the curtains even tighter, got into bed and went to sleep.

But then, there was ANOTHER knock at the door.

'We are three shepherds.'

'Well, what's the matter? Lost your sheep?'

'We've come to see Mary and Joseph.'

'ROUND THE BACK!' said the innkeeper. Then he shut the door, climbed the stairs, got into bed, and went to sleep.

And there was YET ANOTHER knock at the door.

'We are three kings. We've come . . .'

'ROUND THE BACK!!!'

The innkeeper slammed the door, climbed the stairs, and tried to get some sleep . . .

But THEN, just as he was drifting off, he was woken up by a CHORUS OF SINGING!

'RIGHT! THAT DOES IT!'

So he got out of bed, stomped down the stairs, threw open the door, went round the back, stormed into the stable, and was just about to give this MARY AND JOSEPH a piece of his mind when –

'Ssshh!' whispered everybody, 'You'll wake the baby!'

'BABY!' said the innkeeper.

'Yes, a baby has been born this night.'

'Oh REALLY!?' said the innkeeper, looking crossly into the manger.

And just at that moment, suddenly, amazingly, his anger seemed to fly away.

'Oh,' said the innkeeper, 'isn't he lovely!'

In fact, he thought he was so special . . . the innkeeper woke up ALL the guests at the inn, so that they could come and have a look at the baby too.

So no one got much sleep that night!

(Nicholas Allan)

Just as Mary and Joseph struggled to find a roof over their heads that night, so many people find themselves far from their homes at Christmas – perhaps because of work, maybe because they plan to be with other members of the family, or perhaps because there is unhappiness between family members which makes it difficult for them to be together. Sometimes, though, it's just a lack of thought that prevents them realising how much their presence might mean to those who love them.

On the night before Christmas Eve, an elderly man rang up his daughter, Cathy. When she answered, he cut her short with words that shocked her.

'It may be Christmas,' he said with a touch of steel in his voice, 'but enough is enough! Your mother and I have been married for forty-one years and we've finally admitted how much we hate each other. We don't intend to spend one more day under the same roof! We're getting divorced. We can't wait!'

Shocked, Cathy tried to intervene with careful questions and consoling words.

'There's nothing you can say,' he insisted, 'and that goes for your brother too! Tell him the news, will you?'

'Dad, look, I'm going to ring David now! And tell Mum that I'm coming straight up! We need to talk this through. Just *don't do anything* until I get there! Promise?'

'I'm making no promises at all,' replied her dad, before switching off the phone with a flourish.

Five minutes later, David rang his father.

'What's all this about you and Mum?' he demanded. 'Of course you're not getting divorced!'

'It's got nothing to do with you!' snapped his father. 'Your mother and I have decided. That's it!'

'Right, well, I'm collecting Cathy tonight, and we're going to drive straight up together. We'll be there first thing in the morning.'

His dad gave what sounded like a grunt before switching off the phone. Then he turned with a smile to his wife who was standing at his side.

'The kids have decided to come for Christmas! And they're paying their own way . . .!'

Just the Two of Us

So, it's back to just the two of us this Christmas.
It seems hardly worth the bother of it all.
It's not the way it used to be
Back when the kids were small.
The wrapping of the presents,
Filling socks with sweets and toys.
A doll's house for Rebecca,
A train-set for the boys.
There was so much excitement then,
The world seen through their eyes.
The kids awake at four a.m.,
Whispered pleasure and surprise.

But, it's back to just the two of us this Christmas.
Shame the grand-children should live so far away.
We could have bought a Christmas tree,
Played games on Christmas day,
Hung stockings by the fire,
Sung carols at the door,
Watched the kids open their presents,
Wrapping strewn across the floor.
I could have dressed as Santa
Like a festive garden gnome;
But, it's best that little children
Spend their Christmases at home.

So, it's back to just the two of us this Christmas.
Like it used to be before the kids were born.

Christmas Eve

Remember our first Christmas Eve
When we stayed up 'til dawn.
No one else to worry us,
Doing what we liked to do.
Christmas lunch at seven-thirty,
Decorations in the loo.
Drinking mulled wine by the fire,
Midnight service with our friends.
All those special Christmas memories
Wrapped in love that never ends.

Aren't you glad it's just the two of us this Christmas?

(Alan Williams)

Families change over the years. Children grow up and leave to set up homes and start families of their own. Teenagers often don't want to be anywhere but among their own friends and surrounded by their computerised home comforts over the holiday, which means that members of the older generation can feel exhausted at the suggestion of spending Christmas in their noisy, family household where everybody seems busy and preoccupied.

And as time takes its toll – with illness, the aches and pains of getting older, perhaps the shock and sadness of bereavement too – sometimes it's easier to keep Christmas simple. Or maybe not to bother with Christmas at all?

The next poem was written by someone who had obviously felt just like that at times during her life. Her name was Verna Teeuwissen, and she was ninety-three years old when she died in 2004.

We won't have a Christmas this year, you say,
For the children have all gone away,
And the house is so lonely, so quiet and so bare
We couldn't have a Christmas that they didn't share.

We won't have a Christmas this year, you sigh,
For Christmas means things that money must buy.
Misfortunes and illness have robbed us, we fear,
Of the things that we'd need to make Christmas this
  year.

We won't have a Christmas this year, you weep.
For a loved one is gone, and our grief is too deep;
It will be a long time before our hearts heal,
And the spirit of Christmas again we can feel.

But if you lose Christmas when troubles befall,
You never have really had Christmas at all.
For once you've know it, it cannot depart,
When you learn that true Christmas is Christ in your
  heart.

(Verna Teeuwissen, 1911–2004)

Having Christmas in your heart has nothing to do with baubles, turkeys, puddings, cards or present wrapping. In fact, it's when all the niceties of celebration are stripped away that we are brought back to basics – and the bottom line of everything, namely Christ, born on earth, who is also God in heaven.

That deep belief in our redemption through Christ, and the unerring love of our Lord, has kept Christians going through the harshest, most terrifying, painful and hopeless situations down the years. Recently on *Songs of Praise*, I met a wonderful lady called Jane Elgey who, at the age of twelve, had been captured with her mother during the Second World War as they tried to escape from Singapore just as the Japanese invaded after their attack on Pearl Harbor. The 130,000 Allied civilians who were captured during that time included 42,000 women and 40,000 children, most of them Dutch, British or Australian. Jane shared how their faith became even more important to them during their long captivity, which lasted more than three years, during which time many of the women died as a result of the constant hunger and disease.

Jane and her mother were taken to a civilian women's camp in Palembang, Sumatra. Not far away was the men's camp in which many of the women's husbands, friends and relations were housed. No contact was allowed between them, so the only time they caught a glimpse of their men was when the men marched past the women's camp on working parties.

William McDougall, a prisoner in the men's camp, described Christmas 1942 in his book *By Eastern Windows*:

The day before Xmas I marched out with the working party. As usual we began to wave and shout when in sight of the Women's Camp. But the women were silent, standing motionless in the open space . . . Their stillness silenced us. We slowed to a halt and asked each other, in whispers, what was wrong.

The answer came in song. Across the no-man's land which separated us sounded the melody of 'O Come All Ye Faithful'. Our guards were as astonished as we and let us stand there listening. The music softened on the second song, 'Silent Night, Holy Night', and grew stronger on the third, a Dutch carol. Leading the singers was a woman in the habit of a nun. Her arm rose and fell, as though waving a baton.

The guards finally asked us to move on. 'Please walk' they said in Malay. 'Japanese may come.' We walked, moving quietly and slowly in order to hear those voices as long as possible . . .

(William H. McDougall, 1909–88)

O come, all ye faithful,
Joyful and triumphant,
O come ye, O come ye, to Bethlehem.
Come and behold Him,
Born the King of angels:
O come, let us adore Him,
O come, let us adore Him,
O come, let us adore Him,
Christ the Lord.

God of God,
Light of Light,
Lo! he abhors not the Virgin's womb;
Very God,
Begotten not created:
O come . . .

Sing, choirs of angels,
Sing in exultation;
Sing, all ye citizens of heaven above!
Glory to God,
In the highest:
O come . . .

(Latin, traditional)

The Angels

And there were shepherds living out in the fields near by, keeping watch over their flocks at night. An angel of the Lord appeared to them, and the glory of the Lord shone around them, and they were terrified. But the angel said to them, 'Do not be afraid. I bring you good news that will cause great joy for all the people. Today in the town of David a Saviour has been born to you; he is the Messiah, the Lord. This will be a sign to you: you will find a baby wrapped in cloths and lying in a manger.'

Suddenly a great company of the heavenly host appeared with the angel, praising God and saying,

'Glory to God in the highest heaven, and on earth peace to those on whom his favour rests.'

(Luke 2:8-14)

13

Busy Day – Silent Night

Infant holy, infant lowly,
for his bed a cattle stall;
oxen lowing, little knowing,
Christ the babe is Lord of all.
Swift are winging angels singing,
noels ringing, tidings bringing:
Christ the babe is Lord of all.

Flocks were sleeping, shepherds keeping
vigil till the morning new
saw the glory, heard the story,
tidings of a gospel true.
Thus rejoicing, free from sorrow,
praises voicing, greet the morrow:
Christ the babe was born for you.

(Polish traditional carol)

There's something about the build-up and the anticipation as Christmas Eve night approaches that seems to bring out smiles all round. The delicious aroma of mince pies in the oven, Mum in the kitchen stuffing the turkey so it can cook slowly overnight, various bottles and chocolate goodies appearing on sideboards or under the tree, carefully chosen from the list of each family member's favourites, special programmes on television, the usual Christmas hits on the radio – Christmas is coming, and who cares if we get fat!

Christmas certainly can bring out the best in people. In his poem 'At Christmas', Edgar Albert Guest (an Englishman who lived for many years in the United States) muses that it would be wonderful to think that the man of the household, who is not *always* known for his good nature, might find a way to keep the spirit of Christmas all the year round!

At Christmas

A man is at his finest towards the finish of the year;
He is almost what he should be when the Christmas
season's here;
Then he's thinking more of others than he's thought the
months before,
And the laughter of his children is a joy worth toiling
for.
He is less a selfish creature than at any other time;
When the Christmas spirit rules him he comes close to
the sublime.
When it's Christmas man is bigger and is better in his part;
He is keener for the service that is prompted by the heart.

All the petty thoughts and narrow seem to vanish for awhile
And the true reward he's seeking is the glory of a smile.
Then for others he is toiling and somehow it seems to me
That at Christmas he is almost what God wanted him
*   to be.*

If I had to paint a picture of a man I think I'd wait
Till he'd fought his selfish battles and had put aside his
*   hate.*
I'd not catch him at his labours when his thoughts are
*   all of pelf,*
On the long days and the dreary when he's striving for
*   himself.*
I'd not take him when he's sneering, when he's scornful
*   or depressed,*
But I'd look for him at Christmas when he's shining at
*   his best.*

Man is ever in a struggle and he's oft misunderstood;
There are days the worst that's in him is the master of
*   the good,*
But at Christmas kindness rules him and he puts
*   himself aside*
And his petty hates are vanquished and his heart is
*   opened wide.*
Oh, I don't know how to say it, but somehow it seems
*   to me*
That at Christmas man is almost what God sent him
*   here to be.*

(Edgar Guest, 1881–1959)

Women are at their finest at Christmas, too! I sometimes think that mums *make* Christmas! It's not true in every household, of course, and many men are great Christmas planners – but mostly the role falls to the lady of the house. She may huff and puff about it, feeling overworked, under-appreciated and stressed at the looming arrival of visitors and the need to produce meals for so many people – but generally, it is the women of the house who mastermind the whole thing, from presents, cards, shopping and housework to the mammoth job of planning the catering.

So if Mum is feeling a bit harassed and put-upon, she might take comfort in this paraphrasing of the much-loved words of St Paul in 1 Corinthians 13. In the end, no one is going to mind too much if the carpet's not vacuumed, the beds not made up, the kitchen covered in dog hair – and she hasn't had time to get out of her dressing gown yet! What they value and will always remember is the welcome they receive and the love that makes your friends feel like family, and your house feel like home.

1 Corinthians 13 – A Christmas Version

If I decorate the house perfectly with tinsel, cards, strands of twinkling lights and shiny baubles, but do not show love to my family, I'm just another decorator.

If I slave away in the kitchen, bake dozens of mince pies and sausage rolls, pore over recipe books to prepare gourmet dishes, and set the Christmas table so that it looks like something out of a magazine, but do not show love to my family, I'm just another cook.

If I fund-raise for the homeless, sing carols in the local care home for the elderly and take bundles of items down to the charity gift shop, but do not show love to my family, it profits me nothing.

If I trim the tree with shimmering angels and crocheted nativity figures, enjoy Christmas parties and sing in the church choir, but do not focus on Christ, I have missed the point.

Love stops the cooking to hug the child. Love sets aside the decorating to kiss the husband. Love is kind, even when stressed and exhausted. Love doesn't envy the house next door that has co-ordinated Christmas china, table cloth and serviettes.

Love doesn't yell at the kids to get out of the way, but is thankful they are there to be in the way. Love doesn't give only to those who are able to give in return, but rejoices in giving to those who can't.

Love bears all things, believes all things, hopes all things, endures all things. Love never fails. Computer games will crash, necklaces will break, golf clubs will rust – but the gift of love is a blessing forever.

(Sharon Jaynes, adapted)

173

While homes around the world are being made ready for family and friends who are coming to stay for Christmas, others are packing their cases and stuffing brightly wrapped presents into bulky bags which later that night will be under the Christmas tree of whatever household they are travelling to. I love the sheer boyish excitement of this next poem. These lads were travelling home from school a long time ago, but I don't think the thrill of Christmas Eve for children has changed at all! And when you read the second verse about the same boys returning to school after the holiday, it seems that enthusiasm for getting back into the routine of school really hasn't much changed over the years either!

Christmas Holidays

Along the Woodford road there comes a noise
Of wheels, and Mr. Rounding's neat post-chaise
Struggles along, drawn by a pair of bays,
With Reverend Mr. Crow and six small boys,
Who ever and anon declare their joys
With trumping horns and juvenile huzzas,
At going home to spend their Christmas days,
And changing learning's pains for pleasure's toys.

Six weeks elapse, and down the Woodford way
A heavy coach drags six more heavy souls,
But no glad urchins shout, no trumpets bray,
The carriage makes a halt, the gate-bell tolls,

*And little boys walk in as dull and mum
As six new scholars to the Deaf and Dumb!*

(Thomas Hood, 1799–1845)

Of course, some young people can't come home. Military men and women will be on duty in war zones around the world this Christmas Eve, as they have been for centuries.

Just over a hundred years ago, 4 August 1914 saw the start of the First World War across Europe. It was one of the deadliest conflicts in history – 16 million people, both military and civilian, lost their lives, and 20 million more were wounded.

For people who get caught up in war, it can bring out both the very worst and the very best in human nature. And it seems that Christmas, and all it means to those who are far from home, can encourage the human spirit towards fellowship and a deep longing for peace. Derek Dobson wrote the best words in the piece that follows. I filled in with a few others.

Silent Night

It was 1914 – and as the sun rose, it brought little warmth to the icy cold air of the biting wind. The landscape was bleak and battered – battle-worn, just like the exhausted young soldiers who sat or lay along the desolate rows of trenches – the Allies on one side facing their sworn enemies, the Germans on the other.

They'd lost all sense of time as the days had passed – so when someone remembered this was Christmas Eve, it was hard to believe. Christmas Eve had always been spent at home, with stockings and crackers, roast dinner and carols; with Mum and Dad, brothers and sisters; Grandad asleep in front of the fire – and Nan reading from the Bible the much-loved story of the birth of Christ in a humble stable in Bethlehem. How far away that all seemed! How far away they felt from home and God in this hell on earth.

Suddenly, the silence was broken. One lone voice began to sing – *STILLE NACHT, HEILIGE NACHT*. The Allied soldiers realised they knew this song the German was singing – SILENT NIGHT, HOLY NIGHT – and when one of them started to join in, others followed, until their bleak world was filled with singing – no longer enemies, just homesick soldiers remembering the miracle of Christ's birth on that very first Christmas night.

And then, there was movement. A football bounced into No Man's Land between the lines of trenches. An English soldier ran out to kick it, but he was met by a German lad with a fancy line in footwork. Before long, others clambered out, and the match was on!! They cheered and laughed as tension fell away, and they became just boys, friends, playing ball together.

And then, reality dawned. Choking back tears, they hugged one another before sliding back into their own trenches, ready for another day of fighting, to kill, or be killed.

But how wonderful that, for just a short while, in a world torn apart by hatred and war, a song celebrating the birth of the Christ-child brought peace on this troubled earth.

(Derek Dobson)

Stille Nacht, heilige Nacht,
Alles schläft; einsam wacht
Nur das traute hochheilige Paar.
Holder Knabe im lockigen Haar,
Schlaf in himmlischer Ruh!
Schlaf in himmlischer Ruh!

Silent night, Holy night
All is calm, all is bright
Round yon virgin, mother and child
Holy infant, tender and mild
Sleep in heavenly peace,
Sleep in heavenly peace.

Silent night, Holy night
Son of God, love's pure light
Radiant beams from thy holy face
With the dawn of redeeming grace,
Jesus, Lord at thy birth
Jesus, Lord at thy birth.

Silent night, Holy night
Shepherds quake, at the sight

Glories stream from heaven above
Heavenly, hosts sing Hallelujah.
Christ the Saviour is born,
Christ the Saviour is born.

(Joseph Mohr, 1792–1848)

It was only a box of Liquorice Allsorts, but it had me near to tears in the middle of the supermarket on Christmas Eve. For fifty years, I have always bought and wrapped a box of Liquorice Allsorts for my mum at Christmas, and she bought and wrapped an identical box for me.

Then, a few years ago, Mum died. She was in her mid-eighties and had made it quite clear that she was tired, ill and more than ready to go, so in that respect her passing away was almost a welcome relief from the pain and indignity she'd been through in those last awful months. She'd been living with us for four years, so I'd had that wonderful time to get really close to her again – not that closeness was ever something we lacked. Her smile of welcome lit up the room, her sense of humour never dimmed. She was my confidante, my sternest critic, most enthusiastic supporter and simply my best friend. Rarely a day went by in all my life when I didn't speak to her. Suddenly she was gone – and somehow that box of Liquorice Allsorts symbolised the loss. There was no pile of presents under the tree for her now, no stocking to fill, no place at the table – and no box of sweets for her from which I had pinched all the solid liquorice sticks, just as she had pinched all the coconut wheels from the box she gave me!

So here I am, a grown woman with an adult family of my own, feeling bereft and orphaned because my mum is no longer here to talk to, share with, love and be loved by. Her room is simply empty. Her expression in the photo on the wall doesn't break into a sudden smile when I walk in, but remains static and staring. She's gone, and all the hoping in the world can't change that. I find myself burying my nose in her favourite jumper just to be comforted by the familiar smell of her. I chat to her in my mind when I'm bustling around the house, or out in the car – wishing she could hear me, longing for a response. And I can't put into words how much I'd love to be wrapped in one of her hugs again. The longing is a physical hurt. The memory is one of the sweetest I know.

Without her, every Christmas is hard, especially on this Christmas Eve night. I still miss filling her stocking, and holding her hand as we watch *Carols from King's*, which we always loved. I will raise a glass of the homemade ginger cordial that she made on Christmas Eve every year when I was growing up, a tradition which I have followed. And I'll eat her box of Liquorice Allsorts for her, even the pink coconut ones. It's the least I can do.

A note to the whiskery men in your household! On Christmas Eve, does it ever occur to you that you have been through three distinct stages in your life?

Tidings of Comfort and Joy

Stage One: You believe in Father Christmas

Stage Two: You don't believe in Father Christmas

Stage Three: You ARE Father Christmas!

And what's more, as you lock yourself away in a back room while you pore over the assembly instructions for toddler trikes, electronic toys and train sets, it strikes you that Christmas is a bit like a day at the office. You do all the work, and the fat guy with the suit takes all the credit!

Jingle bells, jingle bells,
Jingle all the way,
Oh, what fun it is to ride
In a one-horse open sleigh!
Jingle bells, jingle bells,
Jingle all the way,
Oh, what fun it is to ride in a one-horse open sleigh!

(Traditional)

Children across the world will struggle to get to sleep tonight! Oh, they've all been told that Santa won't come if they are still awake – but they know that if they listen very, very hard, they might just hear the bells on Santa's sleigh as Rudolph whisks him through the sky on his way to leave them a stocking full of presents!

Christmas Everywhere

Everywhere, everywhere, Christmas tonight!
Christmas in lands of the fir-tree and pine,
Christmas in lands of the palm-tree and vine,
Christmas where snow peaks stand solemn and white,
Christmas where cornfields stand sunny and bright.
Everywhere, everywhere, Christmas tonight!

Christmas where children are hopeful and gay,
Christmas where old men are patient and gray,
Christmas where peace, like a dove in his flight,
Broods o'er brave men in the thick of the fight;
Everywhere, everywhere, Christmas tonight!
For the Christ-child who comes is the Master of all;
No palace too great, no cottage too small.

(Phillips Brooks, 1835–93)

Phillips Brooks was the American minister who wrote 'O little town of Bethlehem', after the moving experience of spending Christmas Eve in Bethlehem in 1865. In this delightful little poem, he manages to capture the excitement of children everywhere on Christmas Eve along with the heart of the Christian message.

Someone else who set out to capture the wonder and glory of Christ's birth in verse was Charles Wesley, who wrote a carol called 'Hark, how all the welkin rings' – 'welkin' meaning the arch of the heavens above us. However, his fellow preacher George Whitefield wondered if that word would be generally understood, so he changed the first line – and hence, the great carol 'Hark! the herald angels sing' was born.

When it came to finding a melody to accompany the words, Charles Wesley was very specific. His words needed a slow and solemn tune befitting the grandeur and dignity of the text. But a moment of genius from an English organist led to a melody being partnered with his words in a way that Charles would have thought most unbecoming!

A century after Wesley wrote his carol, Felix Mendelssohn composed a cantata to mark Johann Gutenberg's invention of the printing press. At the time, Mendelssohn commented that he didn't mind how else the melody might go on to be used, as long as it wasn't partnered with sacred words.

Fifteen years later, organist William Cummings realised that Mendelssohn's tune fitted Wesley's words perfectly – and he was right: that combination of words and music propelled this carol to its status today as one of the most-loved in the world. Neither the composer nor the author would have approved, but we definitely do – and it is the perfect carol to welcome Christmas Day!

Hark! The Herald Angels Sing

Hark! the herald angels sing,
'Glory to the newborn King!'
Peace on earth, and mercy mild,
God and sinners reconciled
Joyful, all ye nations, rise,
Join the triumph of the skies;
With the angelic host proclaim,
'Christ is born in Bethlehem.'
Hark! the herald angels sing,
'Glory to the newborn King!'

Christ, by highest heaven adored:
Christ, the everlasting Lord;
Late in time behold him come,
Offspring of the virgin's womb.
Veiled in flesh, the Godhead see;
Hail, the incarnate Deity:
Pleased, as man, with man to dwell,
Jesus, our Emmanuel!
Hark! the herald angels sing,
'Glory to the newborn King!'

Hail! the heaven born Prince of peace!
Hail! the Son of Righteousness!
Light and life to all he brings,
Risen with healing in his wings
Mild he lays his glory by,
Born that man no more may die:

Tidings of Comfort and Joy

Born to raise the sons of earth,
Born to give them second birth.
Hark! the herald angels sing,
'Glory to the newborn King!'

(Charles Wesley, 1707–88)

The Shepherds

When the angels had left them and gone into heaven, the shepherds said to one another, 'Let's go to Bethlehem and see this thing that has happened, which the Lord has told us about.'

So they hurried off and found Mary and Joseph, and the baby, who was lying in the manger. When they had seen him, they spread the word concerning what had been told them about this child, and all who heard it were amazed at what the shepherds said to them. But Mary treasured up all these things and pondered them in her heart. The shepherds returned, glorifying and praising God for all the things they had heard and seen, which were just as they had been told.

(Luke 2:15-20)

14

On Christmas Day in the Morning

Ding dong! merrily on high
In heav'n the bells are ringing.
Ding, dong! verily the sky
Is riv'n with angel singing.
Gloria, Hosanna in excelsis!

E'en so here below, below
Let steeple bells be swungen,
And io, io, io
By priest and people be sungen.
Gloria, Hosanna in excelsis!

Pray ye dutifully prime
Your matin chime, ye ringers,
May ye beautifully rime
Your evetime song, ye singers.
Gloria, Hosanna in excelsis!

(George Ratcliffe Woodward, 1848–1934)

Around the country, bells were rung to call people to midnight services from which they emerge at the very start of Christmas Day. Sleepy now, but warmed and fulfilled by the worship they have just shared, they remember once again the age-old story of Emmanuel – Christ born on earth to redeem our sins, to share our human experience, and to show us by example the loving nature of God. All this was made possible by the obedience of a young mother, Mary, who had been through so much since the visit of the angel nine months earlier.

The Angel of the Lord Declared Unto Mary . . .

People joke about not being able to choose their relatives. But you made your home in my womb and my heart as though they were the safest places to bide winter. It is cold, now, baby Yeshua. The stars are brittle in the sky and the donkey's breath is visible by the light of the lamp hanging from one of the rafters in this barn.

In Galilee, on such nights, a bitter wind sometimes blows in from the lake and makes it difficult to keep the house clean. We are always sweeping away sand and dust. We light fires early in the evening and make bread, eat it while it is still warm. I miss my home. I miss my mother so much I keep crying.

An angel in a dream told Joseph who you are. 'What is conceived in her is from the Holy Spirit,' he said. 'You are to give Him the name Yeshua because he will save His people from their sins,' he said.

When the angel came to see me, such a flood of words gushed from my mouth that I hardly knew myself! 'He has given help to Israel, his servant, mindful of His mercy. Even as he spoke to our fathers, to Abraham and to his posterity forever,' I said.

I know now they were not my words. They were for posterity.

If I gently push my third finger into the centre of your fist, you frown but your tiny fingers curl over my finger-tip. If I bend my face to your head, my lips brush your soft hair, and I breathe in your fragrance. My left arm cradles you and you sleep, satisfied, at my breast.

These are my words.

(Therese Down)

And as Mary nursed her baby, Joseph looked on too. What was he thinking? Were his thoughts altogether more practical as he gazed at the boy who, by being born, had created a family with Mary and Joseph?

I made you a little bed. Proper little bed, all planed smooth with no nasty splinters. I set it on rockers and carved a little lamb on the headboard. You'll see it when we get back to Nazareth. You'll like it. Well, I hope so because I wouldn't like you to think your father wanted you to be born in this old feeding trough. One of the legs is a bit wobbly. Well, that's nails, you see. Never trust nails. That should have been jointed, good and proper. Takes a little care, that's all. And now I've got to take care of you as well. I know who you are, you see. You don't know who I am, though, do you? I've not really had anything to do with you. I wish I was your father – you're so beautiful. But I'm just standing in, as you might say, for someone else . . .

But do you know what I think? I think you are going to have your real father's temperament. Because, you see, your father is a loving, kind, mighty, glorious, everlasting God. And the angel in my dream told me that you are going to save your people from their sins – which does seem a lot of ask of a little chap like you. But I think I shall be pretty proud of you anyway. You're still part of my family, you see. And it's a good family. O yes, we go back a long way. I may only be a carpenter, but your great, great, great, great, great, great grandfather was King. There! He was. King David. We've had kings, priests, farmers, carpenters and now we've got a king again.

(Paul Burbridge and Murray Watts)

The love of Mary and Joseph for their son reminds me of a particularly wonderful experience I had as a parent. It's a golden memory which always warms my heart at this time of year, and it's something that reminds me how it can often be the gift that costs nothing at all that touches your heart most deeply.

I remember a time quite a few years back when our family had been going through a tough patch, and for me that Christmas was tinged with sadness and worry. My children were quite young then, but they still pick up on the atmosphere, don't they? Very late on Christmas Eve, I was wide awake in bed when I heard the sound of soft footsteps creeping downstairs from the attic bedroom above me – and that could only be my son, Max, who was about eleven years old at the time. When I realised he was making for my room, I hardly dared breathe as the door was slowly pushed open. I heard him move across the room to place something heavy and rustling on my feet. Then he crept out, closing the door behind him. When I was sure he was safely back in his room, I switched on the light to see what he'd left. It was an old Christmas stocking that he'd filled with thoughtful treats for me from treasures he'd found around the house – a satsuma and some nuts; Christmas chocolate from the tree; paper hankies; a packet of sweets; sachets of shampoo and hand cream from the bathroom; a biro – and best of all, a card with kisses hoping that I would have a happy Christmas because he knew I'd been sad.

I felt tearful and overwhelmed. His sensitive, loving care made that stocking the *best* present I've ever had, given in the true spirit of Christmas, full of reassurance, promise, hope and blessing. In my son's love, I found myself feeling that God was very close. He'd reminded me that Christmas is not about expensive *presents*, but about the blessings we already have, and the unfailing *presence* of God. In the loneliness of feeling sad, I'd almost forgotten that – and it took the kindness of a young boy to remind me of the *true* meaning of Christmas.

From the moment you open your eyes on Christmas morning, there is something in the air, a sense of anticipation and excitement about the day to come. In our house, that excitement feels extra special because two members of our family have Christmas Day birthdays, which means we have to be sure we make a big fuss of their birthdays, along with the universal celebration of the birth of Christ.

Christmas Thoughts

It's sharing your gifts, not purchasing gifts;
It's not wrapping presents, it's being present
and wrapping your arms around the ones you love;
It's not getting Christmas cards out on time,
It's sending any card, any time, at the right time;
It's not having the biggest and best Christmas light
   display,
It's displaying the Christ light that comes from your
   heart;
It's not Santa coming down the chimney,

On Christmas Day in the Morning

It's Jesus coming down from heaven,
and giving us the gift of eternal life.

(Anonymous)

Are you ever too old for stockings? Apparently not! For us the day starts with Christmas stockings for everyone, whether you're five or fifty! Miraculously, brightly coloured stockings have appeared for each member of the family – sometimes laid across the foot of their bed, sometimes just left outside their door – that's for those who choose to stay up longer than 'Santa' can keep her eyes open! Like most mums I have, of course, been recruited to become one of Santa's elves, a temporary job that runs from the start of December. I have a Christmas grotto all of my own in various places around the house where presents for everyone have been stashed away ready for wrapping. Oh, the wrapping! I've spent several long evenings sitting cross-legged on the floor surrounded by black bags full of gifts which need to be sorted, wrapped, stuck, labelled, and put in the right place for wherever they need to be – taken to the Post Office, put in the 'stocking' bag, or piled under the tree. It can be backbreaking work, and I have nightmare memories of Christmas mornings when I've watched people opening the wrong gifts, and have realised that Santa's elf has obviously got the labels mixed up!

Christmas Pickle

One year I asked for slippers,
And my brother asked for socks.
My sister asked for perfume
And my dad asked for a watch.
Mother only wanted something pretty for her hair,
We checked the list before it went
To make sure all was there.

But . . .

As Santa did his thing
Our list he must have lost,
For underneath the Christmas tree
Our presents were all crossed.
My brother got some slippers,
And I received the watch,
My father opened aftershave
And mother got the socks.
My sister got a pretty bow
She ties up in her hair,
We knew she wanted perfume
But she said she didn't care.

When next Christmas came
We wrote clearly on our list
Just to make sure Santa
Didn't get it in a twist,
But as we opened presents

On Christmas Day in the Morning

We were grateful but confused,
He must have lost our list again
And chaos had ensued.

This year my mum got slippers
And I received the socks.
My brother opened aftershave
And sister got the watch.
My father got a hat
And something pretty for his hair.
We didn't get the things we'd asked
But knew the thought was there.

That time of year is here again,
And we don't like to doubt,
But we write the list all muddled up
And try to catch him out.

But . . .

As we open presents
We cannot help but giggle.
He's got us all mixed up again,
Our gifts are in a pickle.

My mother gets the perfume
So she gives it to my sister.
My sister gives me slippers
And I thank her as I kiss her.
My dad gets socks he doesn't want
And brother gets the watch.

They see their gifts across the room
And then decide to swap.

I receive a pretty bow
To tie up in my hair,
But I give it to my mother
And we all decide that's fair.
We know that Santa's busy
And he's got a lot to send,
And, with a little help from us,
He gets there in the end!

(Bethan Williams)

There's something so intriguing and thrilling about inspecting wrapped Christmas presents. It's hard to resist picking each one up and shaking it to try and work out what treasure it contains. Two days before Christmas last year, our three-year-old grandson, Jacob, managed to grab himself ten vital minutes alone in the lounge with the Christmas tree – and when we discovered him, his expression was a mixture of shock, obvious guilt and feigned innocence as he stood surrounded by a huge pile of ripped Christmas paper and about twenty presents in full view in the middle of the room! The look on his face said, 'It wasn't me, honest!'

Yeah, right!

On Christmas Day in the Morning

It's an odd thing that we spend days making sure the house looks just right for Christmas – and then, in the space of a mad half hour, or perhaps longer depending on the size of the crowd, the floor of the room in which the Christmas tree stands disappears under mounds of paper ripped off by excited children and smiling family and friends. Piles of presents are balanced precariously around the floor, on the arms of settees, and on laps. Jumpers and scarves and gloves are tried on and modelled for all to see. Books are glanced at, jokes shared, cards read out, the size of the money gift on tokens compared between siblings – along with the occasional quiet sigh that a longed-for gift is not there, or the message in a card from someone special was less loving than the recipient had hoped.

The room ends up looking as if a bomb has landed in it – but what a glorious mess it is! I remember one year looking out over all the ripped paper and packaging and realising just how much of it I had wrapped myself, even the presents which bore greetings from that old rascal, Santa Claus! It was at just that moment that my small daughter came up and, with a very concerned expression, asked, 'Did *you* get me anything for Christmas, Mum?'

Anyway, that post-present mess is one of my favourite times of the year, and I never rush to clear it up. Does it matter if we have to tiptoe around a small boy, biting his lip with concentration as he tries to assemble a Lego truck? Or heed a little girl's command to *shush* because her new baby doll is tucked up in a *very* pink pushchair and is trying to get some sleep!

It is good to be children sometimes, and never better than at Christmas when its mighty Founder was a child Himself.

(Charles Dickens)

In our house, there always seems to be a gift of a well-known board game to at least one member of the family, and our plan *before* lunch is that we will play it *afterwards*. But we rarely get round to it – which is hardly surprising as I heard the other day from someone 'in the know' that, on average, even the most popular board game is only ever played 4.7 times! Not only that, but when you think how many jigsaws are given as presents at Christmas, it's a surprise to learn that 97 per cent of them are never finished. I don't feel so bad now I know I'm not alone, and very few other people ever get round to putting in that last piece of blue sky either!

Some presents may cause raised eyebrows. I love this little story from Gervase Phinn in his delightful book *The Virgin Mary's Got Nits*:

I do like bright colours. Red in particular is such a cheerful, uplifting hue. When my wife, Christine, was fifty I bought her some rather attractive lacy red silk underwear for Christmas.

When she opened her present in front of our four grown-up children and my mother, the onlookers turned the very same colour of the said undergarments.

'Put them away, Christine!' snapped my mother. 'His father went through that stage!'

Still, I love the idea that Gervase had thought to give his wife something frivolous and totally unnecessary, which is something most wives really appreciate, even though they may prefer some gifts to be opened in private! We've all had our share of steam cleaners, ironing boards and toolkits as presents when what we really hoped for was the right brand of perfume or gift tokens so that we can choose for ourselves the handbag we *really* would like in the January sales!

In fact, maybe we could all do with thinking more carefully about what we give and why.

Every year Grandma gets a tin of talcum powder.
She always says, 'Ah, my favourite!'
Even before she opens the wrapping.
Grandpa always says, 'Well, I know what's in here.
It's two pairs of socks. Just what I wanted!'

This year, Auntie Vi got an umbrella
In an umbrella-shaped parcel.
I mean, it looks just like an umbrella.
And before Auntie Vi pulled the paper off,
She said to Mum, 'It will match that new coat of mine.'

As for Mum and Dad, they just sat there and said,
'We've given each other a joint present this year.
It's a digital clock radio for our bedroom.'
Do you know, they didn't even bother to wrap it up and
    put it under the tree!

At the end, when everything had been given out,
Mum said, 'We mustn't forget the gift-vouchers from
    Debbie and Jim.
We sent them a cheque for the same amount.
We always do.'
I call that a bit unimaginative, don't you?

Maybe when you come to think of it
Grown-ups need Father Christmas far more than
  children do.

(Roderick Hunt)

All too soon, it's time for me to disappear into the kitchen to organise Christmas lunch. With the family all happily poring over presents or chatting elsewhere in the house, I quite happily get on with whatever needs to be done in the kitchen. That's when I find myself thinking about what has warmed my heart most that morning.

Perhaps it's because I love writing that, for me, the simple gift of *words* is what I really value – when someone writes more than just *Lots of love, Fred and Alice*, in their card, but really gives thought to what they want me to know. Words of love, old friendship and warm memories, encouragement and comfort mean so much when you receive them, and actually feel good when you write them too.

And knowing how the 'cook' in the family rarely seems to leave the kitchen over Christmas, I so appreciate it when those I love come and join me, and give me the gift of their *time*, probably over a cuppa when we laugh, and reminisce about the people we'll always miss. We make time not just to *listen* to each other, but really to *hear* what the other is saying. I don't do enough of that throughout the year, so I want to make sure I give more of my own time, and remember to value and respect other people's time too.

On Christmas Day in the Morning

The gift we all hope and pray for, especially at Christmas, is 'peace on earth' – and I don't think that's going to come about through war or politics, but through each one of us striving for peace in our own corner of the world, in our hearts, our homes and our relationships. We long for God's peace, the true promise of Christmas, and the greatest gift of all with which we were blessed one holy night in Bethlehem.

Once in royal David's city,
Stood a lowly cattle shed,
Where a mother laid her Baby,
In a manger for His bed:
Mary was that mother mild,
Jesus Christ, her little Child.

He came down to earth from heaven,
Who is God and Lord of all,
And His shelter was a stable,
And His cradle was a stall:
With the poor, and mean, and lowly,
Lived on earth our Saviour holy.

For He is our childhood's pattern;
Day by day, like us, He grew;
He was little, weak, and helpless,
Tears and smiles, like us He knew;
And He feeleth for our sadness,
And He shareth in our gladness.

And our eyes at last shall see Him,
Through His own redeeming love;

For that Child so dear and gentle,
Is our Lord in heaven above:
And He leads His children on,
To the place where He is gone.

(Cecil Frances Alexander, 1818–95)

There comes a moment when all the Christmas dishes are served and I've taken off my apron and joined everyone at the table. The crackers have been pulled, jokes laughed at, silly hats placed on heads, a photo taken of the whole family smiling warmly as they sit ready to tuck into their turkey dinner – and I feel myself breathe out with relief and overwhelming love. This is my family, my dearest friends, with whom I share warm memories and unknown futures. *Bless them all, Lord. Fill the hearts of all gathered here with love, courage, hope and peace.*

I find myself thinking how the faces around our table have changed over the years, and I remember with a tinge of sadness my own parents and grandparents who used to share Christmas with us. *May they rest in your care, dear Lord – and know that they are ever loved, valued and missed.*

As I look around the smiling faces, I'm aware of the challenges and concerns facing each of them. That one is starting out on his career and is worried about the future. Will he be able to make a decent living, or will he have to compromise on his dream? That young mum already has a noisy toddler and now she is pregnant again. Will she be able to cope? Will her husband be able to earn enough to support their growing family? That next couple are recently married. Will they grow together in fulfilment and commitment? They sit across from a husband and wife who have been married for years but seem worryingly distant from each other these days – are they unhappy? And the much-loved elderly lady at the end of the table is struggling with her health as the years take their toll. She lives in constant pain, and the strain is deeply etched into the lines of her face. Lastly, I think with sadness about the person who isn't here, but should be – the one who finds family relationships difficult and is not speaking to any of us at the moment. I wonder where she is and whether she is thinking of us, as I know many round this table are thinking of her.

Life can be hard. For each of us in our own way there is worry, struggle and self-doubt. But the bonds between us are deep and unbreakable. In the end, when push comes to shove, we are there for each other. We always will be. That's family. Often infuriating, sometimes frustrating – but bound together by blood and belonging. I thank God for each and every one of them.

Bless us this Christmas, Lord. May we cherish what we have, all who love us, all we love. Grant us the wisdom and courage to make the most of everything we are. Help us to embrace whatever life brings our way with energy and gratitude – and as we recognise how fortunate and blessed we are, may we work with equal commitment to relieve others who struggle just to survive, and reach out to them in your power. And may we take every step with you. Christ beside us. Christ within us. Christ before us. Amen.

Tidings of Comfort and Joy

God bless you all this Christmas Day;
May Bethlehem's star still light thy way
And guide thee to the perfect peace
When every fear and doubt shall cease.
And may thy home such glory know
As did the stable long ago.

(Edgar Albert Guest, 1881–1959)

And the child grew and became strong; he was filled with wisdom, and the grace of God was on him.

(Luke 2:40)

15

The Morning After the Day Before

Joy to the world, the Lord is come!
Let earth receive her King;
Let every heart prepare Him room,
And heav'n and nature sing,
And heav'n and nature sing,
And heav'n, and heav'n, and nature sing.

(Isaac Watts, 1674–1748)

Whereas Christmas Day is triumphant, full-hearted, indulgent and glorious, in many ways Boxing Day is a big sigh of contented relief that the bustle and excitement is now over. For most of us these days, it means the prospect of almost a week of relaxation stretching ahead until New Year is past and we all go back to work. Bliss!

People choose to spend the day in various ways. Brave souls leap into the icy waters along the South Coast. Other courageous folk head for the Boxing Day sales to pick up bargains that are half the price they were *before* Christmas! Perhaps they're getting their Christmas shopping done early for *next* year! There are traditional sporting events to watch, local football matches to play, dogs to walk, and waistlines to slim down after the thoroughly enjoyable excesses of the day before. In fact, the sentiments of Trevor Harvey's poem about Christmas Day may be all too true on Boxing Day too!

Christmas Day Blues

I've no idea what it could be
That's disagreed so much with me.
But it's something that I've eaten –
Perhaps it was the cheese?
Or it could have been the chocolates,
The plate of mushy peas,
The nuts, the quiche, the oranges,
The toast and strawberry jam,
The oven chips, the Brussel sprouts,
The ice cream and meringue,
The yoghurt and bananas,
The pizza, figs and dates,
The mince pies and the vol-au-vents,
The crisps, the fairy cakes,
The jelly and the cornflakes,
The sausage on a stick –
I don't know which of them it was,
But something's made me sick!

(Trevor Harvey)

Hopefully no one I'm cooking for feels *too* full from Christmas itself, because lunch on Boxing Day is my favourite of the whole year. In September, I always bottle up some homemade pickled onions, which are ceremoniously opened on Boxing Day as we sit down to a lunch of all the best leftovers from the Christmas feast. Cold turkey, beef and honey roast ham, along with baked beans and chips. Scrumptious!

The calorie-conscious might say they're only going to have a small salad, but they never do, not when faced with all the favourites that are piled on the table for that wonderful lunch. For me, it's also a chance to have another portion of Christmas pudding, which I enjoy almost as much then as on the previous day when the pud was brought to the table glowing with blue flames from the brandy in which it had been generously soaked. I'm teetotal, actually – I have been ever since I realised I didn't like the taste of alcohol when I first tried it as a teenager – but the alcohol itself is burnt away by the flaming process and what remains is the most gloriously rich and fruity flavour. A portion of that, with lashings of brandy cream, is *the* taste of Christmas for me!

The house is still littered with the evidence of Christmas gifts, wrapping and cards which various members of the family have not quite got round to moving. At that point they are glad that I had a pen and pad handy on Christmas morning when all the present-opening was going on, so that I can remember for all of us exactly what gift has been given by which person. And sometimes Boxing Day is the time when you find yourself thinking properly about what presents you've received, and how appropriate (or otherwise) they are!

Christmas Thank Yous

Dear Auntie
Oh, what a nice jumper
I've always adored powder blue
And fancy you thinking of
Orange and pink for the stripes!
How clever of you!

Dear Uncle
The soap is
Terrific
So useful
And such a kind thought
And how did you guess that
I'd just used the last
Of the soap that last Christmas brought?

Dear Gran
Many thanks for the hankies
Now I really can't wait for the 'flu
And the daisies embroidered
In red round the 'M'
For Michael
How thoughtful of you!

Dear Cousin
What socks!
And the same sort you wear
So you must be the last word in style

The Morning After the Day Before

And I'm certain you're right and the luminous green
Will make me stand out a mile.

Dear Sister
I quite understand your concern
It's a risk sending jam in the post
But I think I've pulled out
All the big bits
Of glass
So it won't taste too sharp
Spread on toast.

Dear Grandad
Don't fret
I'm delighted
So don't think your gift will offend
I'm not at all hurt
That you gave up this year
And just sent me
A fiver to spend.

(Mick Gowar)

All too soon, those lovely days after Christmas are slipping by and plans for New Year celebrations begin to fill our minds. Feelings are often mixed at this time of year. We'll all be a year older. We find ourselves looking back not just at the pleasures of the year past, but at the worries too, wondering if they might just get worse rather than better in the year to come. Will we be able to cope with all that the passing of time brings our way?

New Year is hardest of all for people who find themselves without anyone really close to them with whom to share the opportunities and the fears of whatever lies ahead. While all around are planning parties and gatherings safe in the knowledge that at the stroke of New Year there will be someone there to kiss them and hold them close, for many that minute of mass embracing is the loneliest time of all. Whether you choose to join a party, or watch the occasion from the safety of your own armchair, there is no time when loneliness seems more overwhelming than on New Year's Eve.

Loneliness can engulf people in different ways and for a variety of reasons. Bereavement, divorce, separation, distance, lack of confidence, financial limitations, old arguments, being too busy with work to make time for loving relationships, simply not meeting the 'right' person – the possible reasons are endless, but the feelings are just the same. At any other time of the year, we can keep such feelings buried beneath the stuff of everyday life – but at the stroke of midnight on New Year's Eve, there is nothing lonelier than standing in a crowd of kissing couples when you are on your own. I've been there. Haven't we all? It's an awful feeling and it undermines our confidence in ourselves.

A few years ago when I was feeling very low around New Year, I remember someone saying a couple of things to me that really struck a chord.

The first was 'happiness is a decision'. The more I thought about that, the more I realised it's true. We all go through difficult times, when we feel defeated by life and its problems, but our attitude to those times is key to our ability to move on. It's the old 'glass half full, glass half empty' conundrum. You can either look at your lot in life and feel defeated by all you lack – or you can recognise the abilities and blessings you do have, and *decide* to make the best of them.

The second piece of advice which really hit home for me was 'If you want to change your life, *you* have got to change your life.' What a deceptively simple piece of advice that is! How true, though, that no one else can change our lives for us. That is something we must decide we want, and then act upon.

That realisation is both terrifying and exhilarating – but, as Mark Twain pointed out, you may be even more unhappy with the result of simply making no change at all.

Twenty years from now you will be more disappointed by the things that you didn't do than by the ones you did do. So throw off the bowlines. Sail away from the safe harbour. Catch the trade winds in your sails. Explore. Dream. Discover.

(Mark Twain)

I'm often reminded, as I hear the chimes of Big Ben on the radio before the news, about the true and very moving story that led to them becoming part of our radio-listening history.

Back in December 1917, two comrades at the Front in Palestine talked through the night before a battle. One of them, Major W. Tudor Pole, remembered very well his friend's words:

'I shall not come through this war. You will survive and live to see a greater and more final conflict. When that time comes, remember us who have gone on ahead. We shall be an unseen and mighty army. Give us the chance to pull our weight. You will still have time available as your servant. Lend us a moment of it each day and, through your silence, give us our opportunity. The power of silence is greater than you know. When those tragic days arrive, do not forget us.'

Prophetic words. While Major Pole survived, the following day his friend died.

In 1940, a determined Major Pole wrote to the BBC suggesting that there should be a silent minute while Big Ben struck so that everyone could have their own thoughts. His suggestion came just as the country had been through the terrible months of the Blitz, and, after a lot of discussion, the BBC governors agreed. On Remembrance Sunday 1940, the chimes broadcast just before the nine o'clock evening news had a new meaning for many listeners gathered behind their black-out curtains. Major Pole's comrade had spoken of the power of silence – although some discovered that the words of the Lord's Prayer, said slowly and with care, neatly fitted between the chimes.

I often think of that when I hear church bells ringing or a clock chiming. And on New Year's Eve, before all the hugs and kisses start, what could be better than to take our own silent minute to remember those who have gone before us, our love and appreciation for them, and our hopes for a better future for all.

I wonder how many people who have celebrated well on New Year's Eve wake the next morning with a tinge of regret? The mixture of the party atmosphere, good company and a little too much of the bubbly stuff can loosen tongues and behaviour in a way that might cause regret the day after. I think the concerns of Phyllis McGinley as she tries to recall her lapses of the previous evening might seem alarmingly familiar to many!

Reflections at Dawn

I wish I owned a Dior dress
Made to my order out of satin.
I wish I weighed a little less
And could read Latin.
Had perfect pitch or matching pearls,
A better head for street directions,
And seven daughters, all with curls
And fair complexions.
I wish I'd tan instead of burn.
But most, on all the stars that glisten,

I wish at parties I could learn
to sit and listen.

I wish I didn't talk so much at parties.
It isn't that I want to hear
My voice assaulting every ear,
Uprising loud and firm and clear
Above the cocktail clatter.
It's simply, once a doorbells' rung,
(I've been like this since I was young)
Some madness overtake my tongue
And I begin to chatter.

Buffet, ball, banquet, quilting bee,
Wherever conversation's flowing,
Why must I feel it falls on me
To keep things going?
Though ladies cleverer than I
Can loll in silence, soft and idle,
Whatever topic gallops by,
I seize its bridle,
Hold forth on art, dissect the stage,
Or babble like a kindergart'ner
Of politics till I enrage
My dinner partner.

I wish I didn't talk so much at parties.
When hotly boil the arguments,
Ah? would I had the common sense
To sit demurely on a fence
And let who will be vocal,

The Morning After the Day Before

Instead of plunging in the fray
With my opinions on display
Till all the gentlemen edge away
To catch an early local

Oh! there is many a likely boon
That fate might flip me from her griddle.
I wish that I could sleep till noon
And play the fiddle,
Or dance a tour jete' so light
It would not shake a single straw down.
But when I ponder how last night
I laid the law down.
More than to have the Midas touch
Or critics' praise, however hearty,
I wish I didn't talk so much,
I wish I didn't talk so much,
I wish I didn't talk so much,
When I am at a party.

(Phyllis McGinley, 1905–1978)

The start of a new year always seems so significant as a marker. If we do want to make changes in our life and attitude, then that is surely the time to start. Full of good intentions, we make a list of our New Year resolutions – and, if we're lucky, we may still remember a few of them by the end of January!

For most of us, those resolutions usually centre upon eating less, exercising more, and developing a bit of backbone when it comes to self-control and healthy living. Do the thoughts of the next parody of a well-known Christmas poem sound all too familiar to you?

'Twas the month after Christmas, and all through the house
Nothing would fit me, not even a blouse.
The cookies I'd nibbled, the eggnog I'd taste
All the holiday parties had gone to my waist.
When I got on the scales there arose such a number!
When I walked to the store (less a walk than a lumber).

I'd remember the marvellous meals I'd prepared;
The gravies and sauces and beef nicely rared,
The wine and the rum balls, the bread and the cheese
And the way I'd never said, 'No thank you, please.'
As I dressed myself in my husband's old shirt
And prepared once again to do battle with dirt –
I said to myself, as I only can
'You can't spend a winter disguised as a man!'

So, away with the last of the sour cream dip,
Get rid of the fruit cake, every cracker and chip,
Every last bit of food that I like must be banished
'Till all the additional ounces have vanished.
I won't have a cookie, not even a lick.
I'll want only to chew on a celery stick.

I won't have hot biscuits, or corn bread, or pie,
I'll munch on a carrot and quietly cry.

The Morning After the Day Before

I'm hungry, I'm lonesome, and life is a bore –
But isn't that what January is for?
Unable to giggle, no longer a riot.
Happy New Year – and to all a good diet!

The Magi Visit the Messiah

After Jesus was born in Bethlehem in Judea, during the time of King Herod, Magi from the east came to Jerusalem and asked, 'Where is the one who has been born king of the Jews? We saw his star when it rose and have come to worship him.'

When King Herod heard this he was disturbed, and all Jerusalem with him. When he had called together all the people's chief priests and teachers of the law, he asked them where the Messiah was to be born. 'In Bethlehem in Judea,' they replied, 'for this is what the prophet has written:

'"But you, Bethlehem, in the land of Judah, are by no means least among the rulers of Judah; for out of you will come a ruler who will shepherd my people Israel."'

Then Herod called the Magi secretly and found out from them the exact time the star had appeared. He sent them to Bethlehem and said, 'Go and search carefully for the child. As soon as you find him, report to me, so that I too may go and worship him.'

After they had heard the king, they went on their way, and the star they had seen when it rose went ahead of them until it stopped over the place where the child was. When they saw the star, they were overjoyed. On coming to the house, they saw the child with his mother Mary, and they bowed down and worshipped him. Then they opened their treasures and presented him with gifts of gold, frankincense and myrrh. And having been warned in a dream not to go back to Herod, they returned to their country by another route.

(Matthew 2:1-12)

16

Journeying On

We three kings of Orient are
Bearing gifts we travel afar.
Field and fountain, moor and mountain,
Following yonder star.

O star of wonder, star of night,
Star of royal beauty bright,
Westward leading, still proceeding,
Following yonder star.

(John Henry Hopkins Jr, 1820–91)

The Twelve Days of Christmas actually begin on Christmas night, so that Twelfth Night runs from the evening of 5 January all through the day of 6 January. This is the time of Epiphany, marked by the lighting of candles to remind us of the bright star which led the Three Kings, or Magi, from their homelands many miles to the east in order to bring gifts to the infant Christ. Kaspar, King of Tarshish, brought myrrh, for mortality. The gift from Melchior, King of Numidia, was gold, signifying kingship. Balthazar, King of Chaldea, gave the child frankincense for divinity. According to legend, Joseph used the gold to pay the inn's bill, burned the incense to quell the stable smells and anointed Jesus with myrrh to protect him from disease.

We three kings of Orient are
Bearing gifts we travel afar.
Field and fountain, moor and mountain,
Following yonder star.

Chorus: O star of wonder, star of night,
Star of royal beauty bright,
Westward leading, still proceeding,
Following yonder star.

Born a king on Bethlehem's plain,
Gold I bring to crown Him again,
King forever, ceasing never
Over us all to reign.

Frankincense to offer have I.
Incense owns a Deity nigh.
Prayer and praising all men raising,
Worship Him, God on high.

Myrrh is mine: its bitter perfume
Breathes a life of gathering gloom.
Sorrow, sighing, bleeding, dying,
Sealed in a stone-cold tomb.

Glorious now behold Him arise,
King and God and Sacrifice.

Alleluia, alleluia!
Sounds through the earth and skies.

(John Henry Hopkins Jr, 1820–1891)

In memory of the Kings' journey, many families add the figures of the Magi to their nativity tableau, sometimes moving each one slowly inwards from the corner of the room over the weeks until they reach the crib.

For centuries the Eve of Epiphany, 5 January, was a great night of celebration in this country, with Twelfth Night parties featuring many dark, fruity, traditional cakes decorated with so many candles that the sparkling occasion almost eclipsed Christmas! Hidden in each cake was a dried bean and a pea, and the couple who found them would be crowned King and Queen of the Bean.

Nowadays, the only way we mark Twelfth Night in our homes is by taking down the Christmas decorations, for fear of bad luck if the chore is done too late, because that would mean that they would have to stay up for the rest of the year! So much for the New Year resolution to keep the place tidy and do things on time then!

Well, so that is that. Now we must dismantle the tree,
Putting the decorations back into their cardboard boxes –
Some have got broken – and carrying them up into the
    attic.

The holly and the mistletoe must be taken down and
    burnt,
And the children got ready for school. There are enough
Left-overs to do, warmed up, for the rest of the week –
Not that we have much appetite, having drunk such a
    lot,
Stayed up so late, attempted – quite unsuccessfully –
To love all our relatives, and in general
Grossly overestimated our powers. Once again
As in previous years we have seen the actual Vision and
    failed
To do more than entertain it as an agreeable
Possibility, once again we have sent Him away,
Begging though to remain His disobedient servant,
The promising child who cannot keep His word for
    long.

(W. H. Auden, 1909–73)

Was W. H. Auden right? Have we reduced Christmas to a festival of over-indulgence and merry-making in a way that overlooks the glory at the heart of it all? Perhaps, in the carol that follows, which is said to have come originally from the Tyrol, we may find in the words of children the simple truth that generally we've chosen to overlook as modern life takes over?

*The wise may bring their learning, the rich may bring
     their wealth,*
*And some may bring their greatness, and some bring
     strength and health;*
We, too, would bring our treasures to offer to the King;
*We have no wealth or learning; what shall we children
     bring?*

*We'll bring Him hearts that love Him; we'll bring Him
     thankful praise,*
*And young souls meekly striving to walk in holy
     ways;*
And these shall be the treasures we offer to the King,
*And these are gifts that even the poorest child may
     bring.*

We'll bring the little duties we have to do each day;
*We'll try our best to please Him, at home, at school, at
     play;*
And better are these treasures to offer to our King;
*Than richest gifts without them – yet these a child may
     bring.*

(From *The Book of Praise for Children*, 1881)

It's easy to think that what happened in Bethlehem two thousand years ago is so far removed from us and the world we live

in today that it really isn't relevant any more. But the facts of his birth and the challenges which his family faced are hauntingly familiar in the twenty-first century too.

Lest We Forget at Christmas

Once upon a time, there was born a baby
a baby whose mother was an unmarried teenager
a baby born into poverty and whose birth took place in
*   a shed full of animals and their excrement*
a baby that grew up with many younger brothers and
*   sisters until he left home at the age of 30*
a humble man who chose to be baptised by a poor man
*   who lived in the desert*
a homeless young man without any qualifications and
*   'nowhere to lay his head'*
an unselfish man who was tempted by evil to do wrong
*   and think only of himself*
a compassionate man who wept when his close friend
*   died*
a trusting man who was rejected and betrayed by one
*   of his closest friends*
a kind and caring man who committed no wrong yet
*   became a convicted criminal and imprisoned*
a frightened man who sweated blood when he knew of
*   his impending death*
an innocent man who was brutally and painfully
*   executed by a cowardly judge as his mother looked on*
a man who epitomised love and forgave his
*   executioners as he died for us all*

The man? Jesus, who – thank God – rose from death
and lives today.

(Derek Dobson)

So, thank God for the birth of Jesus in Bethlehem all those centuries ago! Thank God for his life, his teaching, his compassion and his understanding of the human condition. Thank God for Christ's death for us as atonement for all the wrongs we have done and all the thoughtless faults we continue to have. Thank God for Christ's resurrection, which brings redemption to us in the form of God's unending love. And thank God for Christmas, now and always.

The Week After

Thou that diest, Thou that never diest,
Thy day of birth has come and gone again,
Heaven has sung Hosanna in the Highest!
And Earth has sung Peace and Goodwill to men!

And some have feasted, and still more have fasted,
But in the week that now has slipped behind
The movement was a warm one while it lasted,
And the hearts of men were willing to be kind.

Tidings of Comfort and Joy

Oh, keep that movement warm, not only now
But in the weeks that still beyond us lie!
Oh, keep that movement constant in us,
Thou that ever diest, and wilt never die.

(Eleanor Farjeon, 1881–1965)

The Word became flesh and made his dwelling among us. We have seen his glory, the glory of the one and only Son, who came from the Father, full of grace and truth.

(John 1:14)

References

Introduction: Hallelujah or Ho Ho Ho?

'We Wish You a Merry Christmas': a sixteenth-century carol from the West Country set to a traditional folk melody.

Does Christmas Matter?

'Love Came Down at Christmas': Christina Rossetti, 1830–94 (public domain).

When was the First Nowell?

'It Came Upon the Midnight Clear': Edmund Sears, 1810–76 (public domain).

'The Shepherds': Godfrey Rust, from the sequence *The Last Straw* © Godfrey Rust www.wordsout.co.uk. Used with permission.

Sugar and Spice and all Things Nice

'We All Like Figgy Pudding': from 'We Wish You a Merry Christmas', a sixteenth-century carol from the West Country set to a traditional folk melody.

'Into the Basin Put the Plums': traditional rhyme, anonymous.

'To Mrs. K—, On Her Sending Me an English Christmas Plum-Cake at Paris', Helen Maria Williams, 1761–1827 (public domain).

Dashing Through the Snow

'A Visit From St. Nicholas': Clement Clarke Moore, 1779–1863 (public domain).

'Christmas Toys': anonymous, from *Echoes of Glory for the Sunday School Source,* J. F. Kinsey and John McPherson, eds. (LaFayette, Indiana: The Echo Music Company, 1888).

'A Good Time is Coming': anonymous (coolest-holiday-parties.com/short-christmas-poems).

'The Christmas Eve News': Philip Waddell, from *Christmas Jokes, Puzzles and Poems* by Sandy Ransford and Paul Cookson (Macmillan, 2001).

'In The Bleak Mid-winter': Christina Rossetti, 1830–94 (public domain).

'Snowball': Shel Silverstein, from *Falling Up* (HarperCollins, 2006). Used with permission. Administered by Edite Kroll Literary Agency Inc.

'A Christmas Snowflake': Derek Dobson, © Derek Dobson 2006. (www.reflectionsofhope.org). Used by permission.

Light in Our Darkness

'Like a Candle Flame': Graham Kendrick, © 1988 Make Way Music (www.grahamkendrick.co.uk). Used with permission.

'The Fairy on the Christmas Tree': © Dawn Ferrett. Used with permission.

'The Gospel Tree': Tafadzwa Mhondiwa Mugari (poemhunter.com).

'Tomorrow Shall Be My Dancing Day': William Sandys, 1792–1874 (public domain).

The First Winter

'Adam Lay Ybounden': fifteenth century (public domain).

'A Virgin Unspotted': author unknown, mid-seventeenth century (public domain).

'The Fall': Godfrey Rust, from the sequence *The Last Straw* © Godfrey Rust www.wordsout.co.uk. Used with permission.

'Bible Class': Gervase Phinn, from *Twinkle Twinkle Little Stars* (Penguin, 2010).

The Messenger

'Saint John Was Like a Flaming Torch': The Venerable Bede, 673–735, translated by St Cecilia's Abbey, Ryde. © 1976, St Cecilia's Abbey, Ryde. Used with permission.

'On Jordan's Bank the Baptist's Cry': Charles Coffin, 1676–1749 (public domain).

'The Coming': R. S. Thomas, *Collected Poems 1945–1990* (Weidenfeld & Nicolson, 2000). Used by permission of the Orion Publishing Group, London.

People Get Ready

'The Angel Gabriel from Heaven Came': Sabine Baring-Gould, 1834–1924 (public domain).

'May This Christmas Be the First of Many': Nicholas Gordon, © Nicholas Gordon. Used with permission.

'O come, O come, Emmanuel': Latin, twelfth century, translated by John Mason Neale, 1818–66 (public domain).

'Christmas is Coming': traditional (public domain).

'December the First 'til Christmas': anonymous.

'Deck the Halls with Boughs of Holly': American, nineteenth century (public domain).

'The Holly and the Ivy': traditional English folk carol (public domain).

'Mistletoe': Walter de la Mare, from *Collected Rhymes and Verses* (Faber & Faber, 1989) Used by permission of the Literary Trustees of Walter de la Mare and the Society of Authors as their representative.

Let Your Little Light Shine

'Deep in darkness we begin': Andrew Pratt (born 1948). © 2003 Stainer & Bell Ltd, 23 Gruneisen Road, London N3 1DZ, England, www.stainer.co.uk. Reproduced by permission.

'Four Candles': words adapted by Pam Rhodes.

'With this Candle': anonymous.

'Light a Candle': anonymous (familyfriendpoems.com).

'The Advent Virus': anonymous.

'The Spirit of Christmas': anonymous.

'The First Nowell': anonymous (public domain).

Prayers and Presents

'Tell Out, My Soul': Timothy Dudley-Smith (born 1926). © Timothy Dudley-Smith in Europe and Africa. © Hope Publishing Company in the United States of America and the rest of the world. Reproduced by permission of Oxford University Press. All rights reserved.

'The Nativity Play': Gervase Phinn, from *The Day Our Teacher Went Batty* (Puffin, 2002).

'Advent 1955': John Betjeman, from *Collected Poems by John Betjeman* © 1955, 1958, 1962, 1964, 1968, 1970, 1979, 1981, 1982, 2001. (John Murray, 2006). Reproduced by permission of John Murray Press, an imprint of Hodder and Stoughton Limited.

'A Letter To St Nick': Alan Titchmarsh, from *Alan Titchmarsh's Fill My Stocking*. Published by BBC Books. Reprinted by permission of The Random House Group Limited.

'O Little Town of Bethlehem': Phillips Brooks, 1835–93 (public domain).

Laughter and tears

'Away in a Manger': sometimes attributed to John Thomas Macfarland (1851–1913), *Gabriel's Vineyard Songs* (1892 Louisville), *Little Children's Book: For Schools and Families* (1885 Philadelphia) (public domain).

''Twas the Daze Before Christmas': anonymous.

'Three things are required at Christmas time': anonymous.

'Panto!': Lines by Higgs, 2006.

'The Little Match Girl': Hans Christian Andersen, 1805–75 (public domain).

'Remember Them': Pam Brown, from *To Someone Very Special, Merry Christmas!* © Helen Exley 1992. Used with permission of Helen Exley Giftbooks. www.helenexley.com.

'The Joy You Give': John Greenleaf Whittier, 1807–92 (public domain).

Christmas Eve

'Oh, Holy Night': Placide Cappeau, translated and adapted by John Sullivan Dwight (public domain).

'Joe': Hilary Jane Hughes. © Hilary Jane Hughes. Used with permission.

'Jesus' Christmas Party': Nicholas Allan, © Nicholas Allan 2011. Reprinted by permission of A. M. Heath & Co. Ltd.

'Just the Two of Us': Alan Williams, © Alan Williams (Christmastime.com).

'We Won't Have a Christmas This Year': Verna Teeuwissen.

'The Day Before Xmas': William H. McDougall, from *By Eastern Windows* (Arthur Baker, 1951).

'O come, all ye faithful': Latin, eighteenth century, translated by Frederick Oakeley, 1802–80 and others (public domain).

Busy Day – Silent Night

'Infant holy, infant lowly': Polish traditional carol, translated by Edith Margaret Gellibrand, 1885–1933 (public domain).

'At Christmas': Edgar Guest (1881–1959).

'1 Corinthians 13 – a Christmas Version': Sharon Jaynes.

'Christmas Holidays': Thomas Hood, 1799–1845 (public domain).

'Silent Night': Derek Dobson, © Derek Dobson (www.reflection-sofhope.org). Used with permission.

'StilleNacht, Leilige Nacht': Joseph Franz Mohr, 1972–1848, translated by Stopford Augustus Brooke, 1832–1916 and John Freeman Young, 1820–85 (public domain).

'Jingle Bells': originally entitled 'One Horse Open Sleigh', written by James Lord Pierpont in 1857 (public domain).

'Christmas Everywhere': Phillips Brooks, 1835–93 (public domain).

'Hark, the Herald Angels Sing': Charles Wesley, 1707–88 (public domain).

On Christmas Day in the Morning

'Ding Dong! Merrily On High': George Ratcliffe Woodward, 1848–1934 (public domain).
'The Angel of the Lord Declared Unto Many . . .' (Yeshua): Therese Down. © Therese Down. Used with permission.
'I Made You A Little Bed': Paul Burbridge and Murray Watts, from *Red Letter Days* (Hodder & Stoughton, 1986).
'Christmas Thoughts': anonymous.
'Silly Santa': Bethan Williams. © Bethan Williams. Used with permission.
'I Do Like Bright Colours': Gervase Phinn, from *The Virgin Mary's Got Nits* (Hodder & Stoughton, 2014).
'Every Year Grandma Gets a Tin of Talcum Powder': Roderick Hunt.
'Once in Royal David's City': Cecil Frances Alexander, 1818–95 (public domain).
'God Bless You All This Christmas Day': Edgar Guest, 1881–1959.

The Morning After the Day Before

'Joy to the World': Isaac Watts, 1674–1748 (public domain).
'Christmas Day Blues': copyright Trevor Harvey, first published in *Christmas Poems*, (Macmillan 2000) and reprinted by permission of the poet.
'Christmas Thank Yous': Mick Gowar, *Swings and Roundabouts* (HarperCollins, 1985). Reprinted by permission of HarperCollins Publishers Ltd.

'Twenty years from now': Attributed to Mark Twain, 1835–1910 (public domain).

'Reflections at Dawn': Phyllis McGinley, 1905–78.

''Twas the month after Christmas': anonymous.

Journeying On

'We Three Kings of Orient Are', John Henry Hopkins Jnr, 1820–91 (public domain).

'Well, So That Is That': W. H. Auden (1909-73), from 'The Flight Into Egypt', from *For The Time Being* (1944).

'The Wise May Bring Their Learning': anonymous, from *The Book of Praise for Children*, 1881 (public domain).

'Lest We Forget At Christmas': Derek Dobson, © Derek Dobson 2008 (www.reflectionsofhope.org). Used with permission.

'The Week After': Eleanor Farjeon, from *The Children's Bells* (Oxford University Press, 1957). Used by permission of David Higham Associates.

While every effort has been made to trace the owners of copyright material reproduced herein, the author and publishers would like to apologise for any omissions and will be pleased to incorporate missing acknowledgements in any future editions.

List of Extracts

By first line (title in italics if different from first line).

241

Acknowledgements

Heartfelt thanks to the team at **Hodder Faith** for all their help and professionalism – especially **Ian Metcalfe** who had the spark of an idea, then called in **Ruth Roff, Kate Craigie, Rachael Kichenside, Nick Fawcett, Nicky Bull** and **Dominic Gribben** to encourage me along the way. They've been wonderful!

Kathy Dyke, who's had the difficult job of sorting out copyright on all the pieces I've unearthed and wanted to include. While my enthusiasm ran away with me, she kept my feet firmly on the ground – and her smile never dropped once! Thank you, Kathy.

Lili Panagi, my tough-talking agent who is the most warm-hearted and valued friend.

Trevor Smith, friend, colleague – and brilliant sound producer! I couldn't have done this without you, Trev.

Premier Christian Radio, both the production team, and the listeners with whom I've shared favourite Christmas stories for nearly twenty years.

Songs of Praise – all the production teams with whom I've worked on Christmas programmes and events for nearly thirty years, and the congregations around the country who've allowed me to join them to sing carols by candlelight which have been watched by millions of Christians across the world.

Richard Martin, Fox Records, who has been so helpful in sourcing recordings of Christmas music and themes.

John Cushing of the Thursford Christmas Spectacular in Norfolk, who has created a world of Christmas wonder which has enchanted many thousands of people over the years – including me!

John Street and the Stotfold Salvation Army Band – and all the songsters and musicians of the Salvation Army who have brought the story of Christ's birth to our streets every Christmas for 150 years.

To those who have recorded their thoughts on Christmas in poetry and prose down the centuries – the comical rhymes, the thoughtful readings, the inspirational words which have touched our hearts and lifted our souls – thank you.

To my talented friends who have contributed fresh, new material for this collection – especially **Derek Dobson, Therese Down, Hilary Hughes, Andrew Pratt, Godfrey Rust** and **Bethan Williams.**

And a grateful hello to all the churches across Britain who have invited me to share Christmas celebrations with them year after year. Thank you for the fellowship, the glorious music – and the delicious mince pies!

Tidings of Comfort and Joy

Audio CD ISBN: 9781473633292
Audio Digital Download ISBN: 9781473633285

A collection of the most inspiring Christmas carols,
poems and readings with personal reflections by
Pam Rhodes, in audio format.
Read by Pam Rhodes.

Available on Audio CD and
Audio Digital Download.